Foundations

COPYRIGHT

Copyright © October 2023 by Paul de Sousa

Book Cover by Paul de Sousa

First edition 2023

Also by Paul de Sousa

Foundations
Foundations 8-Weeks Bible Course
Foundation 12-Week Bible Course

Standalone
Entrepreneurs Blueprint

To my God and family for all the love, faith, grace, and light.

CONTENTS

FOREWORD

"Foundations" ... is a powerful grace-based church resource that will set up believers, new and old to live in the power of the finished work of Christ as victorious overcoming believers.

Any church leader who's looking to resource their team to equip the saints in building a strong Gospel centered biblical foundation would find "Foundations" to be a practical tool and timeless resource.

~James Monaghan

INTRODUCTION

Why it's vital.

As with many in the Church I have done a full circle of sorts. Being born into Catholicism, and later in my early twenties attending the Pentecostal Church. With a de- tour later into Seven-day Adventism in my late twenties and finally where for the last 20 plus years growing in my understanding of my sonship to all Christ has accomplished on the Cross in several non-denominational churches.

This course is a more in-depth course with an added four weeks. I pray I knew at the very beginning of my walk in and with Christ. It would have saved me a lot of anxiety, anguish, and time. I have taught many, 4-week, 8-week, 12-week, and one-year foundational, disciple- ship or discovery courses over the years. And the usual questions arise. Sometimes in large groups of over a hundred to smaller groups of 4. This is by no means a hard to read. Rather it is for anyone wanting to lay foundation stones firmly within their souls and renew their minds to the gospel truth.

The eternal and fantastic news of the too-good-to-be- true good news of Jesus. Love you all and pray the leading of the Holy Spirit enlightens His truth not only into your mind but your hearts too.

Now let's start week 1.

CHAPTER ONE

THE WORD (Week One)

The Bible is God's revelation of Himself, His LOVE letter and plan for redemption for all of humanity. Religions consists of man's thoughts about God, but the Bible isn't a compilation of men's thoughts—it contains God's thoughts.

We have developed way of thinking based on our upbringing, experiences, circumstances, and the ungodly influences of this world rather than on the Word of God. Satan comes to steal and to deprive us of what God has given by challenging the way we think. This is evident even from his first dealings with mankind. Concerning the dangers of wrong thinking, the apostle Paul said,

But I fear, lest by any means, as the serpent beguiled Eve through his subtlety, so your minds should be corrupted from the simplicity that is in Christ.2 Corinthians 11:3

We hear people talk about "spiritual warfare" in the sense of going out and doing battle in the heavens. This is based in a misunderstanding of a verse that says we are battling evil powers in heavenly, or high, places (Ephesians 6:11-12). Some people have chartered planes so they could "take their prayers to the sky," or they have gone to the top of skyscrapers to do battle "in heaven." That isn't what this scripture is talking about. The battle against the enemy isn't somewhere out in the atmosphere; the battle is right between your ears.

Satan comes at you through thoughts with lies, deception, and distraction. Adding and subtracting from God Word just as with Adam and Eve. We may eat of the fruit of the trees of the garden: But of the fruit of the tree, which is in the midst of the garden, God hath said, Ye shall not eat of it, neither shall ye touch it, lest ye die. Genesis 3:2-3. but you must not eat from the tree of the knowledge of good and evil, for when you eat from it you will certainly die." Genesis 2:17

The problem with what Eve said is that God never said they couldn't touch the fruit; He said don't eat it. This same thing is happening today. Religion has added to the Word of God and nullified it to hand down traditions. It's exactly what Jesus accused the scribes and the Pharisees of doing (Mark 7:13). Religion is always adding rules and regulations to the Word of God. It is saying, "Don't even touch it or you'll die!" Religion creates manmade traditions, and when people break the manmade traditions and don't die, they go ahead and break God's Word also, thinking that everything was just a hoax.

For example, some religious systems today are saying women shouldn't wear makeup or jewellery—which is a misunderstanding of the scripture that says women shouldn't be concerned with outward adorning, but rather be concerned with the beauty of their hearts. The scripture says don't be concerned with the "outward adorning of plaiting the hair, and of wearing of gold, or of putting on of apparel; But let it be the hidden man of the heart..." (1 Peter 3:3-4). If you interpret this to mean that there should be no plaiting of the hair or wearing of gold, then you have to say there shouldn't be any wearing of clothing either.

BEFORE WE LOOK AT HOW to read the bible its vital that we also look at two other aspects. Is the bible trustworthy and how to rightly divide the Word of Truth?

Can we have confidence in the scriptures we have today as accurate?

It the Bible true?

All scripture is given by inspiration of God, and is profitable for doctrine, for reproof, for correction, for instruction in righteousness: That the man of God may be perfect, thoroughly furnished unto all good works. 2 Timothy 3:16-17

When the apostle Peter was getting toward the end of his life, he wrote a letter to believers in which he stressed the inspiration of Scripture and the confidence we can have that God is speaking to us through it. Peter knew that he was going to die shortly, and he was giving final encouragement to the believers. He said,

For we have not followed cunningly devised fables, when we made known unto you the power and coming of our Lord Jesus Christ, but were eyewitnesses of his majesty. For he received from God the Father honour and glory, when there came such a voice to him from the excellent glory, This is my beloved Son, in whom I am well pleased. And this voice which came from heaven we heard, when we were with him in the holy mount. 2 Peter 1:16-18

Peter was saying, "I'm about to die, but I'm going to write these things down so you can always have this to remember." He was making known that the account he gave of Jesus wasn't something he devised on his own. He wasn't just telling stories. The words he had written down were inspired by God, and they told of Peter's experiences.

PETER WRITES,

We have also a more sure word of prophecy; whereunto ye do well that ye take heed, as unto a light that shineth in a dark place, until the day dawn, and the day star arise in your hearts: Knowing this first, that no prophecy of the scripture is of any private interpretation. For the prophecy came not in old time by the will of man: but holy men of God spake as they were moved by the Holy Ghost. 2 Peter 1:19-21

Peter saw Moses and Elijah talk with Jesus on the Mount of Transfiguration. He saw Jesus radiate light, and he heard God speak with an audible voice from heaven and confirm that Jesus was His Son, but he says we have something even better than that—better than seeing with our eyes or hearing with our ears—we have the written Word of God!

Peter clearly states that the Word of God was not written by men—it was not of "any private interpretation." The Holy Spirit inspired men to write the scriptures. The apostle Paul made the same point in his letter to Timothy when he said,

All scripture is given by inspiration of God, and is profitable for doctrine, for reproof, for correction, for instruction in righteousness: That the man of God may be perfect, thoroughly furnished unto all good works. 2 Timothy 3:16-17

The Greek word for "given by inspiration of God" is literally translated "divinely breathed." This clearly states that the Word of God didn't come from the thoughts of men. God breathed His thoughts into men, who then put them in writing. The Bible is not a human book; it's God's book written for men.

"IT WAS THE EVIDENCE from science and history that prompted me to abandon my atheism and become a Christian."

- Lee Strobel

To begin with, the manuscript evidence supporting the New Testament far outstrips any evidence for secular writings of ancient times.

<u>The New Testament documents have more manuscripts, earlier manuscripts, and more abundantly supported manuscripts than the best ten pieces of classical literature combined.</u>

In contrast to the copies of secular histories given, more than 5,600 Greek manuscripts of the New Testament have survived in whole or in part. Those manuscripts vary in age, the more complete having been written within 150 years of the original, with the earliest manuscript portion written within 30 years of the original. (Keep in mind that the New Testament wasn't written as a single book but is composed of many letters written by multiple authors at different times.

From a purely human perspective, the chance for error is increased when a document is copied repeatedly thousands of times. The more times something is copied, the more errors you should see. This is true in the case of secular works, but not with the Bible. The abundance of ancient New Testament manuscripts has been compared and there are very few differences—and they contain no differences whatsoever that contradict the Gospel message of Jesus or the historical facts of Christian faith. Scholars have placed the comparative accuracy between the more than 5,600 manuscripts at 99.5%!

In addition to the Greek copies of the New Testament, there are thousands more copies of New Testament books produced in other languages during the same time frame. In fact, researchers have discovered more than 9,000 copies of New Testament manuscripts in other languages—bringing the total number of manuscripts to well over 14,000. The abundance of ancient manuscripts and the nearness of their composition to the actual events, makes the New Testament the most verifiable document of antiquity.

Not only do we have copies of the scriptures themselves, but leaders in the early Christian church (often called the Church Fathers) wrote prolifically between 90 and 160 A.D. Their familiarity with the New Testament scriptures we still read today is proven by the fact that all but 11 verses from the New Testament are quoted in their writings!

Non-Christians have also given evidence of Jesus as a historical figure in their writings. In 93 A.D., the Jewish historian Flavius Josephus wrote about the persecution and death of James. He said that the Sanhedrin "...brought before them the brother of Jesus, who was called Christ, whose name was James, and some others, [or, some of his companions]; and when he had formed an accusation against them as breakers of the law, he delivered them to be stoned."

The discovery of the Dead Sea Scrolls between 1946 and 1957 in several caves on the shores of the Dead Sea has given us further evidence of the accuracy of the Scriptures that have been handed down to us. Among the Dead Sea Scrolls was an intact copy of the entire book of Isaiah (known as the Great Isaiah Scroll). It is dated at 100 B.C. and is 1000 years older than the copies that were used to compose the book of Isaiah we read in our Bibles today.

Miniscule, with the variations consisting mostly of spelling mistakes and simple copying errors. The discovery of the Dead Sea Scrolls also proves that the

Messianic prophecies we read in Isaiah were written prior to the birth of Jesus, which reinforces the case that Scripture makes for Jesus as the Messiah.

The bottom line is that the Bible has been handed down through the ages with such accuracy that it can't be just a human book. The different copies we have of ancient secular writings have significant differences in them because they were simply copied by men—they weren't inspired and preserved by God.

The Bible, on the other hand, has been supernaturally preserved by God and all of the evidence we have supports that it was written by the inspiration of God. The last words of David, king of Israel and author of the Messianic prophecies in Psalm 22, reveal how the Holy Spirit inspired the men who wrote Scripture. The Word is reliable!

Jesus quoted from the Septuagint, which was a Greek translation of the Hebrew Old Testament, and He equated Scripture with words proceeding from the mouth of God (Matthew 4:4). Jesus' use of Scripture throughout the Gospels also shows that He believed it was the final authority.

Additionally, the apostle Paul hinged the thrust of his letter to the Galatians on the fact that God made His promise to the seed (singular) of Abraham, instead of to his seeds (plural) (Galatians 3:16). Paul made an argument for Jesus as the promised seed of Abraham based on the singular form of one word from a translation of the original Old Testament scripture—which shows that God is well able to preserve the truth in His Word for us, even though translations.

Rightly dividing the Word

It is crucial for every believer, when reading the Bible, to rightly divide the Word, and to clearly separate what belongs to the old covenant of law and what belongs to the new covenant of grace. When people quote Old Testament passages without appropriating the cross of Jesus in their interpretations, they make it seem as though the cross of Jesus Christ made no difference at all, leading to much misunderstanding and misinterpretation of the Bible.

What Jesus did on the cross instituted the new covenant and made the first covenant—the covenant of the law—obsolete (Hebrews 8:13). In this new covenant, Jesus has already fulfilled for us the righteous requirements of the law (Romans 8:3–4), so that we are no longer under law but under grace (Romans 6:14).

Whether interpreting the Old Testament, or the words which Jesus spoke in the four gospels (Matthew, Mark, Luke, and John), let Jesus and His finished work at the cross be the key to unlocking all the precious gems hidden in God's Word. This means that we must read everything in the context of what He came to do and what He accomplished at the cross for us. For example, some things that Jesus said in the four gospels were spoken before the cross—before He had died for our sins—and some were said after the cross—when He had already won our complete forgiveness and rightfully given us His righteousness. It is the latter that applies to us (believers under the new covenant) today. It is not the white paper in the middle of your bible that separates testaments!

In rightly dividing the Word, we also must take note of who Jesus was addressing when He spoke. With the Pharisees, who boasted in their perfect law-keeping, Jesus spoke of the law at its most pristine standard, such that it was impossible for any man to keep.

He did it so that man would come to the end of depending on himself and begin to see that he desperately needs a Saviour (Galatians 3:24). But to the sinners, the prostitutes and tax collectors, He was never harsh, and was full of compassion for them.

Once you understand how powerful this principle of letting Jesus be the key to understanding and applying God's Word to your life is, you will no longer be troubled by obscure passages in the Bible. This is because the Lord has given so many clear, explicit portions of Scripture that declare His favour and blessings over your life in the new covenant.

So how do I Read the Bible?

One way we should not read the Word is by simply using one's finger and whatever scripture it lands on, use it as it is speaking directly to us.

There are several keys to keep in mind while studying the Bible.

1. The Holy Spirit Enables Our Understanding

"But when He, the Spirit of truth, comes, He will guide you into all the truth; for He will not speak on His own initiative, but whatever He hears, He will speak; and He will disclose to you what is to come" (John 16:13).

IF you don't understand ask the Helper (Holy Spirit) to bring you understanding and revelation. The Word confirm the Spirit and the Spirit the Word they will never contradict themselves.

2. Let Scripture Interprets Scripture

"But know this first of all, that no prophecy of Scripture is a matter of one's own interpretation, for no prophecy was ever made by an act of human will, but men moved by the Holy Spirit spoke from God" (2 Peter 1:20–21).

Here is an example Mat 5:17. "Do not think that I have come to abolish the Law or the Prophets; I have not come to abolish them." Many would see this as proof that enforces the Old Covenant Law (including the 10 Commandments) but what they fail to realize is that the verse quoted is not complete. The actual verse reads -"Do not think that I have come to abolish the Law or the Prophets; I have not come to abolish them but to **fulfil** them. Verse 18 reaffirms "For verily I say unto you, Till heaven and earth pass, one jot or one tittle shall in no wise pass from the law, till all be **fulfilled** (accomplished)." Mat 5:18. So to rightly divide the Word of Truth we need to submit a verse to the rest of Scripture. But what does the rest of scripture say. In the book of the Acts, we find a commentary on the word "**fulfil**" as used in Matt. 5:17. Acts 13:15 "The law and the prophets.", vs 20 "Until Samuel the prophet, vs 25 "John **fulfilled** his course.", vs 33 The promise had been "**fulfilled**.", vs 39 "The law of Moses.". To "fulfil" means to reach the end of the prediction. It has been completed – not to repeated. The following passages show clearly how the word is used in the Scriptures "Until the times of the Gentiles be **fulfilled**." (Luke 21:24), "And as John **fulfilled** his course."(Acts 13:25), "What shall be the sigh when all these things shall be **fulfilled**?" (Mark 13:4.),"The voices of the prophets, they have **fulfilled**." (Acts 13:27.), "And when they had fulfilled all that was written of him." (Acts 13: 29.), "The promise which was made unto the fathers, God hath **fulfilled**." (Acts 13: 32-33.).

After this manner, then, Jesus came to **"fulfil"** all that had been written concerning himself -"All things must be **fulfilled**, which were written in the law of Moses, and in the prophets, and in the psalms, concerning me." (Luke 24:44.)

An Interesting point also is that the term heaven and earth was always in reference to the Temple in Jewish writings and tradition. The place where God would meet. Touching heaven and Earth, The Holy of Holies. Today under the new covenant we are the Temple, and the Holy of Hollies for God now indwells ever believer.

3. **Context Unlocks Meaning (Context-Text=Con after all)**

Example. "There is NO God". Psalms 14:1 says, "There is no God". BUT is that what the context implies? No, the context of this verse reads "Fools say in their hearts, 'There is no God.' They are corrupt, they do abominable deeds; there is no one who does good." (Psalm 14:1). Can you see the danger of just pulling a verse out of its context? It can result in saying the exact opposite of what the Scripture says. Taken out of context, this quote says there is no God. But the context around this verse is not saying this at all.

4. **The Original scriptures never had chapters and verses**

The placement of Chapters came about when Stephen Langton, Archbishop of Canterbury in the early 13th century and professor at the University of Paris, added chapter numbers to all the books in 1227AD. They've stuck ever since. In 1551AD, a printer by the name of Robert Stephanus, added verses to the text of the New Testament within the chapter divisions as he was riding on horseback from Paris to Lyons.

5. **Audience**

For instance, is this passage written to the Jew, the Gentile, the Church, the believer, the unbeliever, is it in the past tense, present tense or future tense etc

6. Through the lens of the NEW COVENANT

As pervious discussed under rightly dividing the Word header we should be careful not to mix the Old Covenant with the New Covenant. Not everything written in the Old Testament is old covenant just as not everything written in the new is new covenant. If not, you will not have a clear picture of all that Christ has accomplish on the Cross. After all, the DEATH and RESURRECTION changed everything.......and just as Christ said that Moses and the Prophets spoke of Him, we are to search the Old looking for our saviour no longer looking for the shadows but the substance which is our reality and view all the old through the lens if Christ and His finished works. We are not against the LAW. On the contrary we are for the LAW for the reason it was give. For the unbeliever not, the believer.

Example in what is commonly known as the Lord's Prayer we read in Matthew 6:13 And lead us not into temptation but deliver us from the evil one.' 14 For if you forgive men their trespasses, your Heavenly Father will also forgive you. 15 But if you do not forgive men their trespasses, neither will your Father forgive yours.... We know this is prior (pre-cross) to the new covenant because the Cross and resurrection had not taken place. Now after the Cross Paul the Apostle reminds us in Ephesians 4:3 Instead, be kind to each other, tender-hearted, <u>forgiving one another, just as God through Christ has forgiven you.</u>

No longer is God forgiving us based on how we forgave but we forgive because we are the forgiven.

7. The Ultimate Goal Is to Know Him

The ultimate goal for studying the Bible is not knowledge; or memorising scripture the ultimate goal for studying the Bible is to know God. To see Jesus in every scripture. Both in the new and the old because all scripture speaks of Him.

You examine the Scriptures carefully because you suppose that in them you have eternal life. Yet they testify about me. John 5:39

And having begun from Moses and from all the Prophets, He (Jesus) interpreted to them the things concerning Himself in all the Scriptures. Luke 24:27

There are hundreds if not thousands of proclaiming theologians that are not born again. There are thousand if not hundreds of thousands that can quote the bible, yet they don't know the author of the living <u>Word!</u>

Questions

Question 1. Where is the battle?

Question 2. What does satan do to Gods Word?

Question 3. Complete the following scripture? 2 Timothy 3:16-17 All scripture is given by inspiration of God, and , for reproof, for , for instruction in righteousness: That the man of God may be perfect, thoroughly furnished unto all good works.

Question 4. How many Greek manuscripts are there presently?

Question 5. True or False. The discovery of the dead sea scrolls affirmed the book of Isiah as we have it today?

Question 6. Write down (Hebrews 8:13?

Question 7. Who helps us understand the Bible?

Question 8. In what years were Chapters and verses added to the Bible?

1)

2)

Question 9. Complete the following statement. Context- = Con.

Question 10. What is the ultimate Goal?

———————

"THE PROBLEM IS NOT the absence of evidence but the suppression of it."

Ravi Zacharias

Answers

Answer 1. Between our ears.

Answer 2. He adds and subtracts from it.

Answer 3. 1) Profitable for doctrine. 2) correction.

Answer 4. 5600

Answer 5. T

Answer 6. Hebrew 8:13 When He said, "A new covenant," He has made the first obsolete. But whatever is becoming obsolete and growing old is ready to disappear.

Answer 7. The Holy Spirit

Answer 8. 1) 1227AD 2) 1551AD

Answer 9. Text.

Answer 10. To know Jesus. (God/Him)

CHAPTER TWO

A Promise. A Condition. A Sign.
(week 2)

Covenant Definition. Berith in the original language. Phonetic Spelling:

(ber-eeth') A Noun. A covenant, treaty, agreement, will or testament.

God has always dealt by means of covenants. Beginning with Adam and continuing until the present day, God's covenants with mankind have had specific characteristics. All covenants have a three-pronged structure. They include a promise by God, a condition, and a sign. There are 8 covenants, but the three-main covenant or agreements are the Abrahamic, the Mosaic and the New Covenant.

The Abrahamic Covenant. ABRAHAM

Genesis 15-17 (Everlasting)

Promise—Father of Multitudes (Gen 15:1-5)

Condition—Faith: Abraham believed (Gen 15:6)

Sign—Circumcision (Gen. 17:10-13)

THE COVENANT OF LAW. MOSES

Until the Seed (Jesus) would come Gal 3:19

Promise—A Great Land (Exo 2:24-25)

Condition—Obedience (Exo 19:7-8)

Sign—The Sabbath (Exo 31:12-18 & Exo 20:8-11)

The Law, the old Covenant, or the Mosaic covenant (referred to the first covenant also in the book of Hebrew) was the Ten Commandment Law.

We read in Exodus 34:28 And He wrote on the tablets the words of the covenant, the Ten Commandments. This is repeated in (Deut. 4:13) And He declared to you His covenant which He commanded to you to perform, that is, the Ten Commandments; and He wrote them on two tables of stone. (Also see additional ref: Deut 9:9-12, 15; 10:4; Deut 5:2-22; 1 Kings 8:9, 21)

The Ten Commandment Law was not given before Sinai. Deut. 5:2-3 says, "The Lord our God made a covenant with us in Horeb. The Lord did not make this covenant with our fathers, but with us." Then he gives the Ten Commandments in vrs. 6-22.

The Ten Commandment were given by Angels. Acts 7:53

Thus, the Old Covenant, the Ten Commandments, had a definite beginning and a definite end. Gal. 3:19 clearly states, "The law was added UNTIL the seed should come." The law and the prophets were until John: since that time the kingdom of God is preached, and every man presseth into it." Luke 16:16

If the law worked, then faith would be irrelevant. (see ref. Rom 4:14) The law brings wrath upon those who follow it. (see ref. Rom 4:15) Christians are not under the law. (see ref. Rom 6:14) Christians have been delivered from the law. (see ref. Rom 7:1-6) The law is good, perfect, and holy but cannot help you be good, perfect or holy. (see ref. Rom 7:7-12) The law which promises life only brings death through sin. (see ref. Rom 7:10) The law makes you sinful beyond measure. (see ref. Rom 7:13) The law is weak. (see ref. Rom 8:2-3)

The strength of sin is the law (see ref. 1 Cor 15:56) The law is a ministry of death. (see ref. 2 Cor 3:7) The law is a ministry of condemnation. (see ref. 2 Cor 3:9) The law has no glory at all in comparison with the New Covenant. (see ref. 2 Cor 3:10) The law is fading away. (see ref 2 Cor 3:11) Anywhere the law is preached it produces a mind-hardening and a heart-hardening veil. (see ref. 2

Cor 3:14-15) The law justifies nobody. (see ref. Gal 2:16) Christians are dead to the law. (see ref. Gal 2:19) The law frustrates grace. (see ref. Gal 2:21) To go back to the law after embracing faith is "stupid". (see ref. Gal 3:1)

The law curses all who practice it and fail to do it perfectly. (see ref. Gal 3:10) The law has nothing to do with faith. (see ref. Gal 3:11-12) The law was a curse that Christ redeemed us from. (see ref. Gal 3:13) The law functioned in God's purpose as a temporary covenant from Moses till John the Baptist announced Christ. (see ref. Gal 3:16 & 19, also see... Matt 11:12-13, Luke 16:16) If the law worked God would have used it to save us. (see ref. Gal 3:21) The law was our prison. (see ref. Gal 3:23) The law makes you a slave like Hagar. (see ref. Gal 4:24) Christ has abolished the law which was a wall of hostility (see ref. Ep 2:15)

<u>I am not against the Law. Rather I uphold the magnitude of its truth. I am for the Law for the very reason (purpose,) the Law was given.</u>

Why the Law then? It was added because of transgressions, having been ordained through angels by the agency of a mediator, until the seed would come to whom the promise had been made. (Gal 3:19) Now the law came in to increase sin (Rom 5:20) The law was never given for the purpose of justification (see ref. Gal 3:24, Rom 3:20). It was totally powerless to save. It only showed us our need and pointed us to a Saviour.

The law is only good if used in the right context. (see ref. 1 Tim 1:8) (see next verse for the context) It was made for the unrighteous but not for the righteous. (see ref. 1 Tim 1:9-10)

The law is weak, useless and makes nothing perfect. (see ref. Heb 7:18-19) God has found fault with it and created a better covenant, enacted on better promises. (see ref. Heb 8:7-8) It is obsolete, growing old and ready to vanish. (see ref. Heb 8:13) It is only a shadow of good things to come and will never make someone perfect. (see ref. Heb 10:1)

"There's a big difference between knowing what something says and knowing what it means. Millions of Christians know what the Bible says. But many do not know what it means because that can only be revealed by the Spirit... Man does not need the enlightening ministry of the Holy Spirit to understand the law; the law was given specifically for the natural man.

We need the Holy Spirit to open our minds to the things having to do with the unfathomable riches of His love and grace, those things that God has freely given us" - Bob Gorge

<u>There was a Promise of a new way, a better way, based on better promises!</u>

"I will make a new covenant...NOT like to covenant that I made with their fathers when I took them out of Egypt." Jer 31:31-32

When Christ came, He put an end to the law for righteousness (see ref. Rom. 10:4). Anyone who advocates the keeping of the law for the purpose of right standing with God is going back to an Old Testament system of law that has been abolished (see ref. Rom 7:1-7, Eph 2:15, Heb 7:12-24, Heb 8:6-13) and is making the work of Christ void in his life. In fact, there is not a one text of scripture in the bible ever mentioning that the Law was to be kept by gentiles.

In fact, the opposite is found (see ref. Rom 2:14 and Gal 2:14-18). That doesn't mean the law has passed away. It is easier for heaven and earth to pass away than for the smallest part of the law to fail. The law hasn't failed. It has been fulfilled (see ref. Matt. 5:17).

Christ fulfilled (see ref. Luke 1:68-79) every jot and tittle of the law for us and imputes to us that righteousness is not based on our performance but on our faith in Him. The law was never given for the purpose of justification (see ref. Gal 3:24, Rom 3:20). It was totally powerless to save. It only showed us our need and pointed us to a Saviour.

The Covenant of Grace or New Covenant. Jesus

Promise =Eternal Life to all who believe (John 3:16)

Condition =Faith (Rom 3:21-28)

Sign =The Lord's Supper (I Cor 11:25, Luke 22:20, Mar 14:24) Water baptism (one time event)

The Bible declares that upon Jesus Christ's death (blood must be shed to institute covenant see ref Heb 9:16-22) and resurrection a new covenant was ratified (instituted). Romans makes it clear that under this new covenant we are:

Romans 7:1-6

"released from the law" v. 2 "dead to the law through the body of Christ" v. 4 "Delivered from the law" v. 6 Which law? verse 7 "...For I would not have known covetousness unless the law had said 'Thou shall not covet." (Compare to Exo 20:17 & I Tim. 1:6-11)

2 Cor 3:1-18 gives us a clear understanding on the differences between the old and new covenants.

Old Covenant / New Covenant

"on tables of stone" v. 3 "on the heart" v. 3

"the letter kills" v. 6 "the Spirit gives life" v.6

"was glorious" v.7 "much more glorious" v. 11

"was passing away" v.14 "remains" v.11

"ministry of death and condemnation" v. 7,9 "Ministry of righteousness" v.9

Old Covenant: Man reaching up to God with self-effort to be accepted by God.

New Covenant: God reaching down to man through Jesus Christ with love and acceptance.

<u>If the Old Covenant has been replaced by the New Covenant what about keeping the Commandments of God?</u> as we read in Rev 12:17 and John 14:15?

Let's see what the Author of the Book of Revelations was referring too. After all the bible it the best commentary of itself.

"For this is the love of God that we keep his commandments. And His commandments are not burdensome." 1 John 5:3

"And whatever we ask we receive from Him, because we keep His commandments and do things that are pleasing in His sight. And this is His commandment: that we should believe on the name of His Son Jesus Christ and love one another, as He gave us commandment. Now he who keeps His commandments abides in Him, and He in him." 1 John 3:22-24

Notice also in Acts 15:5 this was the very same question facing the new church. However, in verses 28-29 there is not mention of keeping the Sabbath day or any of the other Ten Commandments. The only mention is in verse 21 and is speaking of those who preach Moses, not Christ. Christians were not holding the sign of the covenant of Moses any longer (Sabbath) nor were they keeping the sign of the Abrahamic covenant, circumcision. (Gal. 5:1-4).

Christians have a New Law!

Now that we are in Christ we no longer live by the Old Covenant, the Ten Commandments. We have a new law, written on our hearts.

"...but through love serve one another. For all the law is fulfilled in one word, even this: You shall love your neighbour as yourself." Gal 5:13-14 and 18

" A new commandment I give to you, that you love one another; as I have loved you, that you also love one another. By this all will know that you are my disciples, if you have love for one another." John 13:34-35

"Love does no harm to a neighbour therefore love is the fulfilment of the law." Rom 13:10

"Let no one judge you...regarding festival or new moon or Sabbaths which are a shadow of thing to come, but the substance is Christ " Col 2:16-17

Those who belong to Christ Jesus have crucified the old man with its passions and desires. Since we live by the Spirit, let us keep in step with the Spirit. (Gal. 5:24-25). For if you love your neighbour will you kill, steal etc. Our motivation has changed through Christ from fear to that of LOVE. Fear of punishment for not keeping the whole mosaic law to out of LOVE we keep HIS commandment (John 15:12).

And this is his commandment, that we believe in the name of his Son Jesus Christ and love one another, just as he has commanded us. 1 John 3:23

Jesus told them, "This is the only work God wants from you: Believe in the one he has sent." John 6:29

Questions

Question 1. Under the Abrahamic covenant what was the sign?

Question 2. Under the Mosaic covenant what was the condition?

Question 3. Under the New Covenant of Grace what is the promise?

Question 4. What is another word for covenant?

Question 5. True or False? The Ten Commandments were given to Abraham?

Question 6. The Ten Commandments was a ministry of? 1) 2)

Question 7. In Romans 13:10 what is the one word that fulfils the Law?

Question 8. When was the New Covenant ratified (put into effect)?

Question 9. Complete the following scripture: 1 John 3:23 And this is his commandment, that we 1) and 2) , just as he has commanded us.

Question 10. What is the Work of God?

<u>Under Law Man Says</u>	<u>Under Grace Christ Says</u>
Look at what I'm doing for you	Look at what I did for you
Look at how I went to church	Look at how I went to Calvary
Look at how I was raised in my denomination	Look at how I was raised from the dead
Look at how I gave my money	Look at how I gave my life
Look at how I confessed my sins	Look at how I took away your sins
Look at how I stood against sin	Look at how I died for your sins
Look at how successful my life was	Look at how successful My death was

Answers

Answer 1. Circumcision.

Answer 2. Obedience.

Answer 3. Eternal life (relationship with the Father the root, living for ever the fruit John 17:3).

Answer 4. Agreement, will or testament.

Answer 5. False.

Answer 6. 1) Death 2) Condemnation.

Answer 7. Love.

Answer 8. At Jesus death and resurrection.

Answer 9. 1) believe in the name of his Son Jesus Christ 2) love one another

Answer 10. Believe in the one he has sent.

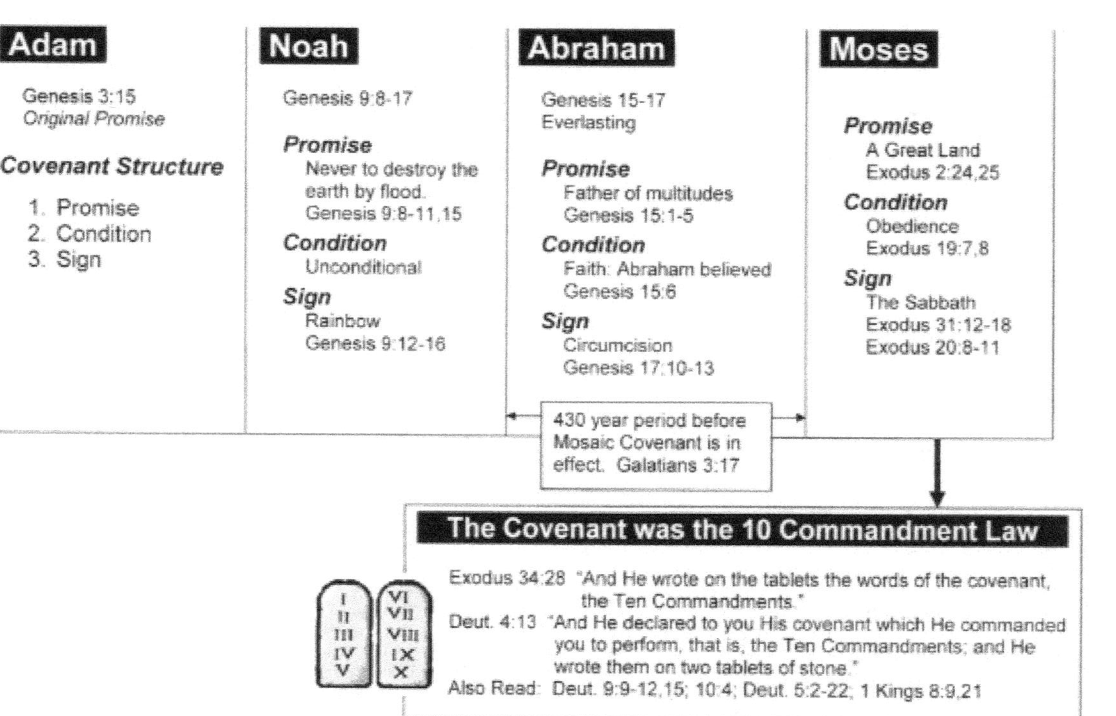

Gospel & Covenants Charts 1

The Old & New Covenants

Jeremiah 31:31,32
"I will make a new covenant…**NOT** like the covenant that I made with their fathers when I took them out of Egypt."

The 10 Commandment Law was never given before Sinai
Deut. **5:2,3** "The Lord our God made a covenant with us in Horeb. **The Lord did not make this covenant with our fathers**, but with us." Then He gives the 10 Commandments in verses 6 to 22.

Abraham

"To Abraham were the promises made… the law was 430 years **later**." Gal. 3:16,17

Moses

The Old Covenant had a definite beginning and end

"The law was added **until** the seed should come." Gal. 3:19

"The seed is Christ." Gal. 3:16

New Covenant
Begins
Matt. 26:26-28
"This is my blood of the New Covenant."

2 Corinthians 3:1-18	
"Old Covenant" v. 14	**"New Covenant"** v. 6
"On tablets of stone" v. 3	"On the heart" v. 3
"The letter kills" v. 6	"The Spirit gives life" v. 6
"Was glorious" v.7	"Much more glorious" v. 11
"Was passing away" v. 13	"Remains" v. 11
"Ministry of death and condemnation" v. 7, 9	"Ministry of righteousness" v. 9

Galatians 4:21-31

"Abraham had two sons: the one by the bondwoman, the other by the freewoman… which things are symbolic. **For these are the two covenants**: the one from Mount Sinai which gives birth to bondage, which is Hagar. For this **Hagar is Mount Sinai**… Nevertheless what does the Scripture say? **Cast out the bondwoman** and her son, for **the son of the bondwoman shall not be heir with the son of the freewoman**. So then, brethren, we are not children of the bondwoman but of the free."

The New Covenant

Moses

"The law was **added until** the seed should come." Gal. 3:19

Promise	Eternal Life to all who **believe.** John 3:16
Condition	Faith. Rom. 3:21-28
Sign	**Baptism.** Col. 2:11-12 **The Lord's Supper.** 1 Cor. 11:25, Luke 22:20, Mark 14:24

Romans 7:1-6

"Released from the law" v. 2
"Dead to the law through the body of Christ." v. 4
"Delivered from the law" v. 6
Which Law? Look at verse 7 and compare with Exodus 20:17. Read also 1 Timothy 1:6-11.

Keeping the Commandments of God

"What about keeping the commandments of God as we read in Revelation 12:17 and John 14:15?"
1 John 5:3 "For this is the love of God that we keep His commandments. And His commandments are not burdensome."

Now read **1 John 3:22-24** "And whatever we ask we receive from Him, because **we keep His commandments** and do things that are pleasing in His sight. And **this is His commandment: that we should believe on the name of His Son Jesus Christ and love one another**, as He gave us commandment. Now he who keeps His commandments abides in Him, and He in him."

Notice also in **Acts 15:5** this was the very same issue facing the new church. But in verses 28, 29 there is no mention of keeping the Sabbath. The only mention is in verse 21 and is speaking of those who preach Moses, not Christ. Christians were not holding the sign of the covenant of Moses any longer (the Sabbath) nor were they keeping the sign of the Abrahamic covenant, circumcision. (Galatians 5:1-4)

A New Law for Christians

Galatians 6:2 "Bear one another's burdens, and so fulfill the **law of Christ.**"
Galatians 5:13,14,18 "...but through love serve one another. For **all the law is fulfilled in one word,** even in this: You shall love your neighbor as yourself."
John 13:34,35 "**A new commandment** I give to you, that you love one another; as I have loved you, that you also **love one another.** By this all will know that you are my disciples, if you have love for one another."
Romans 13:10 "Love does no harm to a neighbor; therefore **love is the fulfillment of the law.**"

Colossians 2:16,17 "Let no one judge you... regarding festival or new moon or **sabbaths,** which **are a shadow** of things to come, but **the substance is of Christ.**"
Note: The LXX (the Septuagint) translation of "Sabbaths" in Exodus 20:8 is the same as Col. 2:16.
Hebrews 3:17-4:11 Christ is the Sabbath rest. A new day, "TODAY" is the gospel rest. Hebrews 4:7
Matthew 11:28 "Come to Me... and **I will give you rest**... you will find rest for your souls."

CHAPTER THREE

The New Covenant. (week 3)

The New Covenant

Many are unaware to the significance of the most talk about human of all time: Christ birth. The World although unbelieving even in the existence of Jesus yet Christ birth is the single event that divides human history into two parts. The world's calendars use Christ's birth to divide history into BC and AD & BC meaning "before Christ" and AD meaning "in the year of our Lord." Even though the world does not recognize Christ the saviour, it does recognize the fact that all of human history centres around Jesus Christ.

However miraculous His birth and the many prophecies regarding His birth, it is in fact <u>His death that is the single most Significant event for all Christianity</u>, God Himself looks at the cross as the dividing line of redemptions plan and on a new way His has choose to deal with all mankind.

You see how He dealt with mankind before the cross is very different from how He deals with you and me today. Before the cross, God dealt with man based on full compliance obedience to the law. Today, God deals with man based on His Love and Grace because of the perfect obedience of Jesus Christ.

The reason for the change is that **Christ's death ushered in a brand-new covenant.** This new covenant that has been prophesied throughout the Old Testament, and the day Christs died, and His blood shed it went into effect as the new way of How God would relate to us.

A covenant is the same as a testament, agreement or will. For a will or covenant to go into effect, the one who made it must die. Most of us understand this from our legal systems. If you have a will, it will not go into effect until you die. This is what the Author of Hebrews bring to light in chapter 9:16-17 tells us: In the case of a will, it is necessary to prove the death of the one who made it, because a will is in force only when somebody has died; it never takes effect while the one who made it is living. Therefore, <u>for the new covenant that God had promised to go into effect, Christ had to die.</u>

The Old Covenant

This new covenant is different from the covenant that God had established with Moses and the nation of Israel at Mt. Sinai. It is not a renewed agreement but a complete new one. After being in bondage and slavery for four hundred years, God led the Israelites out of Egypt and through the Red Sea remember the agreement He had made with Abraham (see ref. Ex 2:24). The Israelites camped at Mt. Sinai and their God gave them the Law. This covenant was a conditional agreement. If they would fully obey Him and keep all the laws He set before them (613 of them), then they would be His treasured possession...and a holy nation (Exodus 19:5,6).

"Then all the people answered together and said, "All that the LORD has spoken we will do." So, Moses brought back the words of the people to the LORD. And the LORD said to Moses, "Behold, I come to you in the thick cloud, that the people may hear when I speak with you and believe you forever." So, Moses told the words of the people to the LORD. Then the LORD said to Moses, "Go to the people and consecrate them today and tomorrow and let them wash their clothes. And let them be ready for the third day.

For on the third day the LORD will come down upon Mount Sinai in the sight of all the people. You shall set bounds for the people all around, saying, 'Take heed to yourselves that you do not go up to the mountain or touch its base. Whoever touches the mountain shall surely be put to death. Not a hand shall touch him, but he shall surely be stoned or shot with an arrow; whether man or beast, he shall not live.' When the trumpet sounds long, they shall come near the mountain."" (Exodus 19:8-13)

Their response reveals man's pride in his belief that he has the ability to produce righteousness. And from that moment forth, God changed His tone, No longer would He be merciful to the murmuring and complaining. No more would He be gracious to speak to them face to face but now behind a veil and through a mediator. The children of Israel should never have changed the covenant that brought them out of Egypt, the Abrahamic agreement. For under the agreement of The Law, the Law will condemn the best of us. As we will see later, this is the purpose of the law in our lives.

To seal this covenant, Moses and the Israelites offered burnt offerings and sacrificed young bulls to the Lord:

When Moses had proclaimed every commandment of the law to all the people, he took the blood of calves, together with water, scarlet wool, and branches of hyssop, and sprinkled the scroll and all the people. He said, "This is the blood of the covenant, which God has commanded you to keep." Hebrews 9:19,20 He declared to you his covenant, the Ten Commandments, which he commanded you to follow and then wrote them on two stone tablets. Duet 4:13, Ex 34:28.

Moses then went back up to the mountain. However, before he could get down to bring the rest of God's commands, the Israelites had already built a golden calf, saying "These are your gods, O Israel, who brought you up out of Egypt" (Exodus 32:4). They could not keep the first commandment. This very commandant they promise to surely do with ease. You see the Israelites could not live up to the covenant. And for the breaking of the agreement the very first day the Law was given 3000 were killed (Ex 32:28). In Duet 28 we see a list of both blessing and curses that was fully dependant on perfect obedience. Twice as many curses for being disobedient.

In number 15:32-36 Moses gives an account of a man that violated the 4th Commandment. "Now while the children of Israel were in the wilderness, they found a man gathering sticks on the Sabbath day. 33 And those who found him gathering sticks brought him to Moses and Aaron, and to all the congregation. 34 They put him under guard, because it had not been explained what should be done to him." 35 Then the Lord said to Moses, "The man must surely be put to death; all the congregation shall stone him with stones outside the camp." 36 So, as the Lord commanded Moses, all the congregation brought him outside the camp and stoned him with stones, and he died.

The law demands perfection and is unbending or immoveable. Because we are all born in sin, it is impossible for anyone to live up to the righteous requirements of the law. But God's intent was not for us to try to live up to the law. His intent was to show us our sinfulness and our need for salvation. And this is all the Old Covenant can show us. It is like a mirror; it can show you the dirt on your face but is unable to clean it. There is nothing wrong with the law. Paul the Apostle wrote, the law is holy, and the commandment is holy righteous and good (Romans 7:10).

The problem was not the Law. The problem is with us. As Hebrews 8:7 says, For if there had been nothing wrong with that first covenant, no place would have been sought for another. But God found fault with the people.

While teaching about God's holy nature, the law also revealed how unholy and unrighteous man is. Paul explained his own experience:

Indeed, I would not have known what sin was except through the law. For I would not have known what coveting really was if the law had not said, "Do not covet". But sin, seizing the opportunity afforded by the commandment, produced in me every kind of covetous desire... Romans 7:7,8

Therefore, no one will be declared righteous in His sight by observing the law; rather, through the law, we become conscious of sin. Romans 3:20

The Law is Holy but when it flows through man's sinful flesh, it shows just how utterly sinful we truly are. The Law is holy, but it cannot make us holy. The Law reveals who we are, but it cannot remove our blemishes. We simply cannot live up to the stringent unbending requirements of the law.

Paul the Apostle discovered something else about the law; "the very commandment that was intended to bring life actually brought death" (Romans 7:12). Coupled with the commandments is punishment for a violation. Under the law, the punishment for sin is death: For the wages of sin is death (Romans 6:23). Because of this there is no hope under this old covenant. It is impossible to keep, the more we tried the more I failed. It condemned us. That's what the Old Covenant did to man. It revealed our sinful nature and showed us how far we are from God's standard of holiness that we would need a saviour.

This is why Paul described the old covenant as the ministry of condemnation, and the ministry that brought death (2 Cor. 3). It was a covenant that required man to live up to its righteous standards, and to those who failed it said, the wages of sin is death. Because man could not live up to the requirements of the old covenant, he experienced fear, shame, condemnation and guilt, and the result was one could never draw near to God.

That is where the Old Mosaic Covenant leaves us but God had spoken of a new covenant coming. In Jeremiah 31 verse 31-32 "The day is coming," says the Lord, "when I will make a new covenant with the people of Israel and Judah. This covenant will not be like the one I made with their ancestors when I took them by the hand and brought them out of the land of Egypt. Something way better was coming. The writer of Hebrews puts it this way:

<u>The former regulation is set aside because it was weak and useless (for the law made nothing perfect), and a better hope is introduced, by which we draw near to God</u>. Hebrews 7:18,19

The Old vs. The New

That 'better hope' is found in the New Covenant. In contrast to the Old Covenant, it is a covenant of grace (God unmerited and undeserving Favour), not of law. The following passage of scripture will help us to see the differences between the two.

The law is only a shadow of the good things that are coming – not the realities themselves. For this reason, it can never, by the same sacrifices repeated endlessly year after year, make perfect those who draw near to worship. If it could, would they not have stopped being offered? For the worshipers would have been cleansed once for all and would no longer have felt guilty for their sins.

But those sacrifices are an annual reminder of sins, because it is impossible for the blood of bulls and goats to take away sins. Hebrews 10:1-4

The Forgiveness of sins under the Old Covenant was a <u>good news/bad news situation</u>. Each year, on the Day of Atonement, the High Priest entered the most Holy of Holies to sprinkle the blood of a bull on the mercy seat to cover the sins of the people committed during the previous year.

Then two goats were sacrificed. One was slain at the altar, the other served as the scapegoat. The sins of the people were transferred symbolically to the scapegoat. And then it was driven out of the city, out into the wilderness, symbolizing the removal of the people's sins. That was the good news.

The bad news was that the next day a person's sins began adding up again. Next year, another sacrifice. Year after year, after year...

God graciously gave this system to Israel as a means for them to experience some relief from their guilt. These sacrifices only covered sins but they could not take them away. Under the Old Covenant, man could enjoy the blessing of God's forgiveness, but that system provided no final solution.

That is why the law is only a shadow. It is a picture of Christ and His finished work on our behalf. It was not the reality. Once you have the real thing, there is no longer a need to focus on the picture. Under the New Covenant, Jesus died for sin once for all. He did not cover our sins like the sacrifices under the law did. He was the Lamb of God who took away our sins.

Therefore, when Christ came into the world, He said: "Sacrifice and offering you did not desire, but a body you prepared for Me; with burnt offerings and sin offerings you were not pleased.

Then I said, 'Here I am' it is written about Me in the scroll I have come to do your will, O God." First he said, "Sacrifices and offerings, burnt offerings and sin offerings you did not desire, nor were you pleased with them" (although the law required them to be made). Then he said, "Here I am, I have come to do Your will." He sets aside the first to establish the second. Hebrews 10:5-9

Although the law required sin offerings to be made, they could never pay the price for sin all they could do was cover them for a year. In order for sin to be fully paid for and taken away, there had to be a perfect payment, a perfect sacrifice from a perfect lamb. This is why Christ came into the world. He offered Himself as a spotless lamb that would take away the sin of the world. As a result, there is no longer any need to offer sacrifices. God has set aside the first covenant to establish a new and better covenant.

And by that will, we have been made holy through the sacrifice of the body of Jesus Christ once for all. Day after day every priest stands and performs his religious duties; again, and again he offers the same sacrifices, which can never take away sins. But when this priest had offered for all time one sacrifice for sins, he sat down at the right hand of God. Since that time, he waits for His enemies to be made his footstool, because by one sacrifice he has made perfect forever... Hebrews 10:10-14

One thing you would never find in an Old Testament temple is a chair. The reason is that a priest's job was never finished. Since the sacrifices offered could never take away sin, they had to continually be offered to keep covering sins. But when Christ offered Himself once and for all, He said, "It is finished." He then sat down at the right hand of God. We have been made holy and perfect forever through His final sacrifice. There is nothing left to offer God as a payment for sin.

The Holy Spirit also testified to us about this. First, he says: "This is the covenant I will make with them after that time, says the Lord. I will put my laws in their hearts, and I will write them on their minds." Then he adds: "Their sins and lawless acts I will remember no more." And where these have been forgiven, there is no longer any sacrifice for sin. Hebrews 10:15-18

The Old Covenant provided animal sacrifices that served as an annual reminder of sins and led to death. Christ's death ushered in the New Covenant. He died in our place to take God's punishment for our sins. As a result, God remembers our sins no more. The sin issue has been settled with God. No other sacrifice is required to gain more forgiveness. We have everything we need under this new covenant. Jesus Christ has done it all.

Sadly, most of Christendom fails to see this and questions still arise. Is the Church still under the old Law covenant. This very say question was asked and answered in Acts 15 at the Jerusalem council.

Remember earlier on the Day of Pentecost when God gave the Law, 3000 people died. But when the Holy Spirit came on the Day of Pentecost 3000 people were saved. (see ref acts 2:40)

CHAPTER FOUR

SALVATION (week 4)

<u>How are we saved?</u>

The basis for salvation.

Paul the Apostle gives us the basis for salvation in Ephesians 2:8-9 Lets read what it says, "For it is by free grace (God's unmerited favour) that you are saved (delivered from judgment *and* made partakers of Christ's salvation) through [your] faith. And this [salvation] is not of yourselves [of your own doing, it came not through your own striving], but it is the gift of God; Not because of works [not the fulfilment of the Law's demands], lest any man should boast. [It is not the result of what anyone can possibly do, so no one can pride himself in it or take glory to himself.]" AMPC

Eph 2:8-9 states that the BASIS of our salvation is **Grace**-that is, God's undeserved and unmerited favour towards us which empowers us as expressed in providing redemption (salvation) through Christ Jesus. The WAY (means) of God saving us is through faith. Through faith we accept God's free gift of salvation which was provided by grace. So, we are saved "by grace through faith". And not by Works so no man can boast. Not by any sort of self-effort, performance or law keeping. Now I know a lot of what I'm going to be saying will sound radical, maybe even heresy to some. But please read on and study the scripture for yourself.

God's grace has already provided all spiritual blessings in Christ (ref. Eph. 1:3) and our faith reaches out to God and receives the benefits (ref. Rom. 5:2).

Simply put **GRACE MAKES** and **FAITH TAKES**. Kenneth S. Wuest translates Ephesians 2:8-9 like this, "For by grace have you been saved in time past completely, through faith, with the result that your salvation persists through present time; and this (salvation) is not from you as a source. Notice that we are not saved by grace alone. We are saved by grace through faith. Faith grants us access to God's grace (ref. Rom. 5:2). Without faith, God's grace is wasted and without grace, faith is powerless. Faith in God's grace has to be released to receive what God has provided through Christ. God's grace is the same towards everyone. Titus 2:11 says, "For the grace of God that bringeth salvation hath appeared to all men." Therefore, all men (mankind) have had forgiveness provided for them (ref. 1 John. 2:2) and extended towards them by God's grace, but not all men are saved. Why? Because not everyone has mixed faith with what God has done for them by grace.

Grace is Gods undeserved, unmerited favour which empowers us from its overflow!

Andrew Wommack explains it perfectly in my view, "Just as sodium and chloride are poisonous by themselves, so grace or faith used independently of each other are deadly. But when you mix sodium and chloride together in the proper way, you get salt, which you must have to live. Likewise, putting faith in what God has already provided by grace is the key to victorious Christian living."

Extreme views of both grace and faith has led to many a false doctrine. Some people emphasize God's grace to an extreme which renders our faith useless. They say everything is up to God's grace and is controlled sovereignly by Him alone. That's wrong. It's just as wrong to emphasize faith apart from God's grace. That's legalism. Faith doesn't move God. God moves of His own free will by grace and faith only appropriates (takes hold of) what God has already provided through His grace. In fact, God is not the one stuck!

Our salvation is not of ourselves or of our doing. It's all Gods doing. It is the gift of God. That is certainly a true statement. However, it is also true that the faith we use for salvation is not of ourselves. It is the gift of God too. There is a human faith and a supernatural, God kind of faith. Human faith is based on physical things that we can see, taste, hear, smell, or feel. God's kind of faith believes independently of physical circumstances (Rom. 4:17). To receive God's gift of salvation, we have to use this supernatural, God kind of faith which isn't limited by our five senses. This is because, to be saved, we must believe on the one we can't see or feel. Human faith can't believe what it can't see. To receive God's gift of salvation, we have to receive the supernatural, God kind of faith first. Where does this faith come from? How do we get it? Romans 10:17 says, "So then faith cometh by hearing, and hearing by the word of God." **God's Word contains His faith**. As we hear the Word of God about our salvation, God's faith comes so that we can believe the good news of our salvation. We actually use God's faith to get saved.

This God kind of faith doesn't leave us after the born-again experience. We never lose this supernatural faith. We just have to renew our minds to the fact that God's faith is in us and then learn how to release it (ref. Rom. 12:3). Eph. 2:8: Salvation is described as a gift. When someone gives you a present you don't ask, "How much do I owe you?"

Your only response should be, "Thank you and open it up" But sadly many Christians after receiving the gift of salvation are still thinking they must work to pay for their acceptance. The only acceptable response to salvation is gratitude (**WOW**) and praise (**THANK YOU**) to God for His indescribable gift (ref. 2 Cor. 9:15). Salvation is a gift to be received (ref. Rom. 6:23), <u>not a wage to be earned</u>. It excludes man's boasting (ref. Rom. 3:27). No one deserves salvation. It cannot be earned by what the Bible calls "dead works" (Heb. 6:1; 9:14). Dead works include all religious activities, good deeds, works of the law, or charity that one may do as a means of being justified before God. Faith towards God and what He has done through Christ Jesus is the only means of receiving His free gift of salvation.

The word "saved" (*sozo*) in the Bible and you will find that it covers forgiveness, healing, preserved, made whole and deliverance. Salvation (soteria from soter = Savior)

Faith is being certain trusting, <u>believing</u>, leaning on the finished work of Jesus!

What about works to be made right with God?

Justification (being made right with God) by works!

James 2:24 which reads, "Ye see then how that by works a man is justified, and not by faith only." KVJ.

The context of the scripture is vital. Our justification *before God* and *before our fellow men* are not the same. Before God we are justified by faith *without works* (ref. Rom. 3:28; 4:5, 6). Before men we are justified *by works* and not by faith only (ref. James 2:24). As soon as the sinner accepts Christ by faith, his name is inscribed in the Lamb's book of life and sealed by the holy spirit into the body of Christ (ref. Eph 1:13). But in order to join the church on earth, something more than faith is required. He must show his faith by his works. Before heaven he is justified *by faith*. Before men he is justified *by works*. Failure to understand the difference between justification before God and man has occasioned much misunderstanding to the point that Luther proclaimed that James should not be in the cannon of scripture. Paul declares that man is justified by faith. James says he is justified by works. Unless we understand that one is speaking of justification before God, and the other of justification before men, James would appear to flatly contradict Paul. But they were writing about different issues. Paul is concerned with the question, "How should man be in right standing (be made right or justified) with God?"

In Romans 3 he says that the whole world stands guilty "before God," and that by works no man can be "justified in His sight" (ref Romans 3:19-20). Then in the next chapter he continues, "If <u>Abraham were justified by works, he hath whereof to glory; but not before God</u>." Rom. 4:2. It is therefore clear that Paul is dealing with justification "**before God**" — right standing "in His sight." James on the other hand is addresses himself to another problem. Here were professed believers hearing the Word without doing it. They were failing to bring forth the fruit of practical godliness. This was revealed in their attitude to their fellow men.

So, the apostle declared: "What doth it profit, my brethren, though a man say he hath faith, and have not works? Can faith save him?

If a brother or sister be naked, and destitute of daily food, and one of you say unto them, Depart in peace, be ye warmed and filled; not withstanding ye give them not those things which are needful to the body; what doth it profit? Even so faith, if it hath not works, is dead, being alone. Yea, a man may say, Thou hast faith, and I have works: shew me thy faith without works, and I will shew thee my faith by my works." James 2:14-18.

Notice that James is dealing with the matter of *showing* his faith:" . . . I will show thee my faith by my works." If "faith" yields no fruit, it is not faith at all, but a counterfeit. So, James continues: "Thou believest that there is one God; thou doest well: the devils also believe, and tremble. But wilt thou know, O vain man, that faith without works is dead? Was not Abraham our father justified by works, when he had offered Isaac his son upon the altar? Seest thou how faith wrought with his works, and by works was faith made perfect? And the scripture was fulfilled which saith, Abraham believed God, and it was imputed unto him for righteousness: and he was called the Friend of God. Ye see then how that by works a man is justified, and not by faith only." James 2:19-24. In his justification with God, Abraham believed God, and that was counted unto him for righteousness.

Romans 2:13 "For it is not those who hear the law who are righteous in God's sight, but it is those who obey the law who will be declared righteous."

At first glance this seems to contradict everything I said earlier (context is required). Apostle Paul elsewhere says about the law he says "it condemns, not justifies" and righteousness "it's a gift and cannot be earned". I Paul the Apostle own words, "Know that a man is not justified by observing the law, but by faith in Jesus Christ." (Gal 2:16) "...if righteousness could be gained through the law, Christ died for nothing!" (Gal 2:21) Is Paul the Apostle sending us a mixed message or is he just skitzo.

Is Paul the Apostle sending a mixed message to the Romans also, for he goes on to conclude: "...that a man is justified by faith apart from the deeds of the law." (Romans 3:28)

The right way to interpret Paul the Apostle in Romans 2:13 is, "having the law is not enough, you have to keep it, and keep it all. All 613 of them – and none of you can!" you see, it`s impossible for imperfect man to deliver a lifetime of perfect performance. Paul the Apostle is not calling us to attempt the impossible; he's trying to get us to face reality and admit defeat. There is no hope for those who try to keep the law: "Therefore, by the deeds of the law no flesh will be justified in His sight..." (Rom 3:20)

Why is failure the inevitable consequence of trying to do the right thing? Because the law is perfect and we're not! We're born sinners on account of the first Adam. We're not sinners because we sin; we sin because we're operating in unprofitable flesh and living in a corrupt and polluted world! The law doesn't generate sin, it merely reveals that we have a problem much bigger than we can solve. "...the law came, so that the full power of sin could be seen." (ref Romans 5:20 CEV) But thank God for "last Adam" Jesus, the man from heaven, is not part of Adam's sinful race. Jesus was the only one who could keep the law and He did so on our behalf. This was the reason He came: "Do not think that I came to destroy the Law and the Prophets. I did not come to destroy but to <u>fulfil</u>" (Mt 5:17) and fulfil He did.

The thirteenth chapter of the Acts of the Apostles is a commentary on "fulfil" as used in Matt. 5:17:

Acts 13:15 "The law and the prophets."

Acts 13:20 "Until Samuel the prophet."

Acts 13:25 "John fulfilled his course."

Acts 13:33 The promise had been "fulfilled."

Acts 13:39 "The law of Moses."

Fulfil. — To "fulfil" means to reach the end of the prediction. Same word in the original language.

"Until the times of the Gentiles be fulfilled." (Luke 21:24.)

"And as John fulfilled his course." (Acts 13:25)

"What shall be the sigh when all these things shall be fulfilled?" (Mark 13:4.)

"The voices of the prophets, . . . they have fulfilled." (Acts 13:27.)

"And when they had fulfilled all that was written of him." (Acts 13:29.)

"The promise which was made unto the fathers, God hath fulfilled." (Acts 13: 32, 33.)

After this manner, then, Jesus came to "fulfil" all that had been written concerning himself. "All things must be fulfilled, which were written in the law of Moses, and in the prophets, and in the psalms, concerning me." (Luke 24:44.)

And he fulfilled them all. He did not come as a destroyer, He came as a fulfiller.

So, we see to trust in any human work, law keeping or effort as a means of salvation is to fall from grace and to sever oneself from the Saviour (Gal. 5:4). No one can be saved by the combination of grace and works, for they exclude each other (Rom. 11:6). You must be saved by grace through faith alone (v. 8) or your works must meet the standard of God's perfection set down by His holy law (Rom. 2:13). "Therefore, we conclude that a man is justified by faith without the deeds of the law" (Rom. 3:28; Gal. 2:16).

Grace and faith eliminate man's boasting altogether (Rom. 3:27). Salvation by grace brings praise and glory to God. If we could save ourselves, either partially or wholly, we would take the credit for it. But that is not the case. All the glory goes to God. Eph. 2:10: There is a vast difference between being saved by good works and being saved UNTO good works as stated here. Good works do not gain us salvation, but they do affirm that salvation has been received into one's life. Good works cannot produce a new nature, but a new nature should produce good work.

Our old history ends with the Cross; our new history begins with the resurrection. — Watchman Nee

QUESTIONS

Question 1. True or False. Grace is Gods merited favour .

Question 2. How do we accept Gods free gift of salvation?

Question 3. Compete the following statement. Grace, faith .

Question 4. Are all men saved?

Question 5. Why?

Question 6. True or false. God is moved by my faith.

Question 7. What are some examples of dead work?

Question 8. Read Galatians 2:16. How are we justified? How are we not justified?

Question 9. Read Romans 3:8. What is its conclusion?

Question 10. Our response to salvation is and praise to God for His indescribable gift.

Question 11. What does the Word fulfil mean?

Additional scripture reading

-In Him we have redemption through His blood, the forgiveness of our trespasses, according to the riches of His grace Eph 1:7

-But by His doing you are in Christ Jesus, who became to us wisdom from God, and righteousness and Holiness, and redemption, 1 Cor 1:30

-who is given as a pledge of our inheritance, with a view to the redemption of God's own possession, to the praise of His glory. Eph 1:14

-how much more will the blood of Christ, who through the eternal Spirit offered Himself without blemish to God, cleanse your conscience from dead works to serve the living God? For this reason, He is the mediator of a new covenant, so that, since a death has taken place for the redemption of the transgressions that were committed under the first covenant, those who have been called may receive the promise of the eternal inheritance. Heb 9:14-15

Answers

Answers 1. False

Answers 2. Through faith

Answers 3. Makes. Takes.

Answers 4. No.

Answers 5. Because not everyone has mixed it with Faith.

Answers 6. False

Answers 7. Religious activities, good deeds, works of the law or charity.

Answers 8. By faith. By observing the Law.

Answers 9. That a man is justified by faith apart from the deeds of the law.

Answers 10. Our response to salvation is gratitude (**WOW**) and praise (**THANK YOU**) to God for His indescribable gift.

Question 11. It means to reach the end of the prediction.

CHAPTER FIVE

Grace (week 5)

<u>Before we see what Grace is, let us have a look to see what Grace is not.</u>

"Grace is cheap." God forbid no, just because something is free doesn't mean it's cheap. Grace and righteousness are free to us, but they were purchased at a priceless expense—the precious blood of Jesus.

"Grace is a license to sin." No, (see ref. Jude 1:3, 4) As born-again Christians, we have received the abundance of grace and the gift of righteousness. We rule and reign in life (Rom 5:17). We have been called to freedom however, we should not allow our freedom to be an incentive to the flesh. The *flesh* is a way of thinking that goes against God (Gal 5:13, *AMP*). Sin has no dominion over us; we are no longer under the Law, but under grace (Rom 6:1-2, 14). The grace of God teaches us to deny ungodliness (Titus 2:11, 12). We should not go halfway, but go all the way, in servitude to righteousness where there is safety (Rom 6:12-13).

"Grace is a license to become lazy or passive." No, the phrase *resting in God* does not describe inactivity. Resting in God describes our determination to trust God while working hard not in activity. When we are doing what God has graced us to do, we want to labour even more (1 Cor 15:10). God is at work in us, giving us the desire to do what He has called us to do (Phil 2:12-13).

"Grace is an encouragement to settle for whatever life throughs at us." No, God will strengthen us in bad situations and circumstances, but He also gives us the grace to improve our circumstances. Jesus never said we would not have trouble in this world, what He did promise is that He will always be with us and that He has already overcome the world. We begin in Him makes that true of us also. He is able to make all grace, every favour, and earthly blessing come to us in abundance (2 Corinthians 9:8, *AMP*). There is a grace to help us succeed and remain victorious no matter what we face.

"Grace is a prayer at mealtime." No, although it's a good thing to thank the Lord for the bounty, grace is not a prayer.

"Grace is non-transforming." No, Grace it's the antidote and true grace is transformation. For the grace of God has appeared, bringing salvation to all men,instructing us to deny ungodliness and worldly desires and to live sensibly, righteously and godly in the present age. Titus 2:11-12

"Grace is just one aspect of the whole council of God." No, In Acts 20:27 Paul the Apostle told the Ephesians "I have not hesitated to proclaim to you the whole counsel of God". Some translations say, the whole "will" of God. The whole counsel and the whole gospel are the same thing. He answers this for us so that there is no confusion three verses earlier:

I consider my life worth nothing to me, if only I may finish the race and complete the task the Lord Jesus has given me—the task of testifying to *the gospel of God's grace*. (Acts 20:24)

The whole counsel of God is the unmixed gospel of His Grace. Simply put:

Jesus plus nothing equates everything!

Definition of Grace.

Grace is defined biblically as God, unmerited, underserving favour. Some have suggested that it is also Gods empowering ability. All though this is true it is not the root but the fruit (or result) of Grace as it overflows from within, being made right with God through the finished work of the Cross. In the Original language it is the word" Charis."

Grace is a person. Jesus!

Grace is not a theology. It is not a subject matter. It is not a doctrine. It is a person, and His name is Jesus. That's the reason the Lord wants you to receive the abundance of Grace, for to have the abundance of Grace is to have the abundance of Jesus. (Joseph Prince, *Destined to Reign*, p.24)

Jesus is Grace personified, and when we accept what He did for us on the cross, we begin to change from the inside out. In the Old Testament, the Law required that the priests continually work to atone for the people's sin. But the perfect one-time sacrifice (see ref. Heb 10:12-14) Jesus made once and for all abolished the need for us to work (perform) to achieve righteousness (right standing). All we really need to do is believe in God's favour toward us. (see ref. Rom 4:1-8).

LET'S DO A COMPARISON!

1. The gospel of grace *is* the gospel of Jesus (Acts 20:24, 2 Th 1:8).
2. We are saved by grace (Eph 2:5); we are saved by Jesus (2 Tim 1:9).
3. We are justified by grace (Rom 3:24); we are justified by Jesus (Rom 4:25).
4. Here are two Biblical blessings that say the same thing: "The Lord be with you" and "grace be with you" (2 Tim 4:22, Phm 1:25).
5. God's grace offers salvation to all (Tit 2:11); Jesus is the Saviour of all (1 Tim 4:10).
6. God is love and love that stoop (or comes down) is grace; Jesus is the Father's love come down (John 16:28).
7. The Holy Spirit is the Spirit of Christ (Rom 8:9) and the Spirit of Grace (Heb 10:29).
8. All the blessings of God come to us by grace alone and all of them are found in Jesus (Eph 1:3).
9. Grace is a teacher (Tit 2:12); Jesus is a teacher (Matt 8:19).
10. Grace reigns (Rom 5:21); Jesus reigns (1 Cor 15:25).

There are many more but it's clear to see. Grace and Jesus are synonymous. Grace is a Person who loves you, died for you, and now lives for you. The <u>gospel of grace is the gospel of Jesus</u> – there is no difference.

"Grace is God as heart surgeon, cracking open your chest, removing your heart—poisoned as it is with pride and pain—and replacing it with His own. Rather than tell you to change, He creates the change. Do you clean up so He can accept you? No, He accepts you and begins cleaning you up. His dream isn't just to get you into heaven but to get heaven into you." — Max Lucado

For I am not ashamed of **the gospel of Christ: for it is the power of God unto salvation** *to everyone that believeth; to the Jew first, and also to the Greek. Romans 1:16*

In the lesson on salvation, we learnt that there is more to the meaning of the word_salvation in the original language. And with in that one can interject the other meaning into this scripture, just as we saw that Grace and Jesus are synonymous.

For I am not ashamed of **the gospel of Grace (Christ): for it is the power of God unto salvation (forgiveness, healing, preserved, made whole and deliverance)** *to everyone that believeth; to the Jew first, and also to the Greek. Romans 1:16*

This is reaffirmed in Galatians 1:6-9 by Paul the Apostle, "I am amazed that you are so quickly deserting Him who called you by **the grace of Christ**, <u>for a different gospel</u>; which is *not* another; only there are some who are disturbing you and want to distort **the gospel of Christ**.But even if we, or an angel from heaven, should preach to you a gospel contrary to what we have preached to you, he is to be accursed! As we have said before, so I say again now, if any man is preaching to you a gospel contrary to what you received, he is to be accursed!

The Power of God is the over the top too good to be true news of Jesus!

Grace wants to infuse our lives with such joy and power that we *know* for certain that it's God at work. He gives us the peace of mind knowing that our salvation is through Him, and not from anything we do. The promise of true freedom through Him remains unchanged (see ref. Psalm 119:45; Rom 6:22)

The Gospel of His Grace.

We just read earlier Why Paul the Apostle was not ashamed of the Gospel of Grace (Christ) in that it is the power of God unto all we need. Acts 20:24

and Galatians 1:6 both use the terms *"gospel "*and *"grace"* interchangeably. In Romans 1:17 we read *For therein is the righteousness of God revealed from faith to faith: as it is written, The just shall live by faith.*

Did you notice that righteousness is not revealed from Law to Law, from good work to good work—it is revealed from faith to faith. What this is say is that: **Sin won't stop the power of God for salvation in your life but trusting in your own good works, self-effort or attempts at law keeping will.** In a previous lesson we learnt that we receive the righteousness (right standing) of God by grace through faith period (Eph. 2:8)! This means that God won't withdraw His power because of sin in your life.

Now I know what you must be thinking, because I was thinking the very same thing when I received this revelation <u>"Well, what about sin?</u> This sounds like you're just giving people a license to sin." No! People have been sinning *without* a license!

We not advocating sin, sinning is stupid and carries consequence. But not with God. Sin is a non-issue with God. The immediate reaction when you start talking about righteousness by faith. Many think you need to make people aware of their sin and the wrath of God. But that's why Paul the Apostle clearly had this question come up that he states in the very next verses Romans 1:18-19 (brackets mine)

For the wrath of God is [already] *revealed from heaven against all ungodliness and unrighteousness of men, who hold the truth in unrighteousness; Because that which may be known of God is manifest in them; for God hath shewed it unto them.*

Notice it says it's manifest *in* them, not *to* them, for God has shown it unto them. **God has put *in* every single person an intuitive knowledge that they are a sinner and that they deserve rejection instead of acceptance.** You don't need to tell people this; they already know it.

"We aren't called to convict people of their sin but to convince them that the only way they can obtain righteousness, or right standing, with God is

through putting faith in what Jesus did for them, not through something they've done." Andrew Wommack

Let's look at Luke 18:9-14 to verify this:

And he spake this parable unto certain which trusted in themselves that they were righteous, and despised others: [10] Two men went up into the temple to pray; the one a Pharisee, and the other a publican. [11] The Pharisee stood and prayed thus with himself, God, I thank thee, that I am not as other men are, extortioners, unjust, adulterers, or even as this publican. [12] I fast twice in the week, I give tithes of all that I possess. [13] And the publican, standing afar off, would not lift up so much as his eyes unto heaven, but smote upon his breast, saying, God be merciful to me a sinner. [14] I tell you, this man went down to his house justified rather than the other: for every one that exalteth himself shall be abased; and he that humbleth himself shall be exalted.

Which are you like the Pharisee or the publican? I'm not talking about your actions but your trust. Do you trust in what you do for the Lord or what He has done for you?

If a person is putting faith in all of their religious acts—all of their acts of holiness—then that will actually *block* them from right standing and relationship with the Father. But the person who maybe hasn't been as good, yet they've humbled themselves and cried out to God, this is the one who enters into right standing with God.

That's what Paul the Apostle tell us in Romans 9:30-32:

What does all this mean? Even though the Gentiles were not trying to follow God's standards, they were made right with God. And it was by faith that this took place. But the people of Israel, who tried so hard to get right with God by keeping the law, never succeeded. Why not? Because they were trying to get right with God by keeping the law instead of by trusting in him. They stumbled over the great rock in their path.

You, see there are **two types of righteousness:** a faith righteousness and a righteousness that comes by the Law. Righteousness by the Law is a righteousness based on performance. Another way to say it is "self-righteousness." The truth is, nobody can perform well enough to get Law righteousness, because the Bible says in Isaiah 64:6 that *"all our righteousness's are as filthy rags."* And James 2:10 and Galatians 5:3 says that if you keep the Law and yet offend in one point, you are guilty of breaking the entire thing. In other words, if you did ninety-nine out of a hundred things right and one thing wrong, according to the Law of righteousness, you would be unrighteous. BUT! If you put your faith in Jesus, you would receive His righteousness—faith righteousness—even though you managed to keep 612 out of the 613 laws. You failed because in God eyes you have broken all!

You could have more holy acts than anyone you know, but who wants to be the best sinner who ever went to hell? All have sinned and come short of the glory of God (see ref. Rom. 3:23).

The over the-top-too-good-to-be-true news is that Jesus imputed our unrighteousness (that's mercy) at His death and imparted His very own righteousness to us at His resurrection (that's Grace).

<u>That's the simplicity of the Gospel. It's all about Jesus so no one can boast in their self-efforts or law keeping!</u>

"Well, I believe in Jesus, but I believe I also have to live holy to be accepted by God."

That's saying Jesus' payment for sin wasn't enough—that you have to add to what Jesus has done—because the Cross did not work and Jesus shedding His blood was worthless! I know it's harsh and you might not say it but that is what it means.

Jesus either paid *for* it all, or He paid for *nothing* at all! It's not Jesus *plus* you; it's Jesus *or* you!

It's not you do the best you can and then Jesus making up the difference with grace and mercy. If you try to mix the two, you have made what Jesus has done of no effect (see ref. Gal 5:4).

It's either by faith righteousness or by your righteousness, but it cannot be a combination of the two (see ref. Rom. 11:6)

"The Church is not an enforcer of rules, but an outpost of Grace."

Brian Houston

Questions

Question 1. True or False. Grace is a licence to sin?

Question 2. True or False. Grace is a prayer before mealtime?

Question 3. Who is Grace?

Question 4. The Gospel of Christ is the Gospel of

Question 5. Complete the Following scripture? In Romans 1:17 we read *For therein is the righteousness of God revealed 1) as it is written, The just 2)* .

Question 6. What will stop the power of God?

Question 7. What will not stop the power of God?

Question 8. Name the two types of righteousness?

1)

2)

Question 9. Read Hebrew 9:12. What did Jesus blood obtain for us?

Question 10. Read Hebrews 13:20 What sort of covenant do we have?

Additional reading.

Under the New Covenant of grace that Jesus put into effect at His resurrection, right standing with God comes by means of a free gift to everyone who will believe (Rom. 4:3-5, 5:18). Yet the faith to believe is tied to the knowledge we have (2 Pet. 1:3-4). If we think our performance is a qualification for God's blessing, we will be sorely disappointed. Because the requirements of the Law are unflexing. It's all or nothing. Either or none. But this is where the good news of the gospel comes in. God doesn't need our ability, just our positive response to His ability.

Hebrews 10:1-2 and Romans 8:1 says that because of the sacrifice of Jesus, we should have no more consciousness of sin. God isn't holding our sins against us because Jesus took care of the sin issue, The Cross worked. In truth God has not only forgiven our sins but also forgotten them. Our slate is clean, and we have been made white as snow but sadly most Christians haven't realized this truth. They are still conscious of their sins, but God isn't.

"Behold, days are coming," declares the Lord, "when I will make a new covenant with the house of Israel and with the house of Judah,not like the covenant which I made with their fathers in the day I took them by the hand to bring them out of the land of Egypt, My covenant which they broke, although I was a husband to them," declares the Lord. "But this is the covenant which I will make with the house of Israel after those days," declares the Lord, "I will put My law within them and on their heart, I will write it; and I will be their God, and they shall be My people. They will not teach again, each man his neighbour and each man his brother, saying, 'Know the Lord,' for they will all know Me, from the least of them to the greatest of them," declares the Lord, "for I will forgive their iniquity, and their sin I will remember no more." Jeremiah 31:34

Blessed is the one whose sin the Lord will never count against them." Romans 4;8 Palms 32:2

Answers

Answer 1. False.

Answer 2. False

Answer 3. Jesus.

Answer 4. Grace.

Answer 5. 1) faith to faith. 2). Live by faith.

Answer 6. Trusting in your own good works, self-effort or attempts at law keeping will.

Answer 7. Sin.

Answer 8. 1) faith righteousness 2) a righteousness that comes by the Law.

Answer 9. Eternal redemption.

Answer 10. An eternal Covenant.

Remember the Law is absolutely inflexible. And Grace absolutely indispensable.

For if you break the law, the law will absolutely break you.

CHAPTER SIX

Faith (week 6)

The Biblical definition for faith is found in Hebrews 11:1, "Now faith is the substance of things hoped for, the evidence of things not seen." Kvj

"Now faith is the assurance (the confirmation, the title deed) of the things [we] hope for, being the proof of things [we] do not see *and* the conviction of their reality [faith perceiving as real fact what is not revealed to the senses]." AMPC

Strong's concordance defines faith as belief, trust, confidence; fidelity, faithfulness in other words certainty in what He has said. More accurately faith (Pistis pronounced {pis'-tis} in the original) literal definition is be *persuaded* and come to trust. It`s also a noun meaning a people, place, or thing. Faith is not work, faith is a rest. Remember Faith is a noun, not a verb. Faith is a persuasion that God is who he says he is, has done what he said he's done, and will do what he has promised to do. Let us consider Abraham, who...

...did not waver through unbelief regarding the promise of God, but was strengthened in his faith and gave glory to God, <u>being fully persuaded</u> that God had power to do what he had promised. (Rom 4:20-21)

Faith is being fully persuaded (certain). When you are fully persuaded, you can rest. The issue is settled you can take God at His Word. Your mind is made up and your heart is at ease. Faith is not a formula.

"Faith is having a good opinion of God. That God is a good God. He is not a taker but a giver."

Joseph Prince

Faith and repentance go together just as Grace and faith do. Grace through Faith is at the centre of the entire Christian walk of bearing fruit. Faith will cause the power of God to come into manifestation, but it isn't because God is responding to your faith. Faith doesn't move God. It moves you into a potion to receive what Grace has already freely provided. In other words, Faith is our positive response to God's grace. "Believe and be saved" (Acts 16:31, Rom 10:9)

Before faith came, we were all under the Law. Now that faith has come, we are no longer under the Law (Galatians 3:23, 25). Faith is a person, and that Person is Jesus. We are saved through faith, which is a gift from God (Ephesians 2:8). Jesus is the Source and object (for no better word) of our faith.

In Matthew 9:27-31 we read the encounter of two blind men receiving healing from Jesus. Jesus asked them if they believed HE was able to heal them.

There response was "yes" then Jesus said, "be it done unto you according to your faith." Jesus did not do the believing for them. They looked to Jesus the Author and finisher of their faith.

"We access Grace by faith." through whom we have gained access by faith into this grace in which we now stand. And we boast in the hope of the glory of God. Romans 5:2

"So how does faith come." Romans 10:7 says," Faith comes by hearing and hearing by the Word." We need Continually hearing the Word of truth: Jesus. Did you know there are two times in all of scripture where Jesus, yes Jesus marvelled at someone's "great faith." We will look at the one. For Jesus who is the author and finisher of our faith to marvel means much. So, let's take a closer look. The story of the centurion is found in Luke 7 and Mark 6. The centurion had a sick servant, so he sent for Jesus, but before Jesus arrived, the centurion came out and told Jesus not to trouble Himself and just say the word and his servant would be healed, He believed the word spoken by Jesus was sufficient to produce the miracle he needed.

"Faith requires action." In the story of the man at the pool of Bethesda (ref John 5) Jesus posed a question. He asked, "Would you like to be made whole" he's response was "yes.". Jesus then commanded him to do what looked imposable in the nature "get up, pick up your bed and walk." This was an act of faith. Most of the time, people took a simple step of faith just by coming to Jesus, yet in this instance Jesus approached the man so the man had no step of faith. Jesus stirred up some kind of faith response in him. Because healing does not come without some manifestation of faith on the part of the recipient, you see Jesus often told people to do something to demonstrate their faith. We see Matt 12:9-13 another example of this were Jesus told the man with the withered hand to "stretch out you hand." And it was after he had stretched out his arm he was healed.

True faith doesn't deny physical truth; it just refuses to let physical truth dominate spiritual truth. True faith subdues physical truth to the reality of spiritual truth.

"Faith speaks." God is the originator of all creation, and the Word of God says that this world was created through His Word (Hebrews 11:3). As offspring of God, created in His image and likeness, we are supposed to be using our words to call those things that be not as though they were and pull unseen things out of the spiritual realm into the natural realm. However, we must grab hold of the fact that words are spiritual containers that carry faith or fear. When you speak the Word of God, you release the faith and power of God into the atmosphere of this earth and create an avenue through which the grace of God can flow into circumstances and situations. "... for out of the abundance of the heart the mouth speaks." Matthew 12:34

And since we have the same spirit of faith, according to what is written, "I believed and therefore I spoke," we also believe and therefore speak (2 Corinthians 4:13)

That if you confess with your mouth the Lord Jesus and believe in your heart that God has raised Him from the dead, you will be saved. For with the heart one believes unto righteousness, and with the mouth confession is made unto salvation. Romans 10:9-10

We get saved by believing (the over-the-top good news of God's Grace: Jesus) in our hearts and giving voice by agreeing with God (confessing) to what we believe.

"Faith is a gift." The good news of Jesus comes wrapped in faith (Rom 10:17). Unwrap the gift of grace and you are left with faith lying all over the place. Grace declares, "It is finished, the work is done," and faith responds, "Thank you, Jesus!" Ephesian 2:8 God saved you by his grace when you believed. And you can't take credit for this; it is a gift from God.

<u>Faith is not something you must do or manufacture. Faith is resting in the restful persuasion that God is at rest and in him so are we.</u>

"We are justified by faith." Romans 4:5 says, "But to him who does not work but believes on Him who justifies the ungodly, his faith is accounted for righteousness." When we fail, don't run away from God. Run boldly to Him, knowing that you are justified by the blood of Christ and not by your good behaviour. The devil may say to you, "How can you do that? Who do you think you are?" Don't listen to him. Pick yourself up and thank God for the blood and the gift of no condemnation. (Romans 8:1) If God justifies the ungodly, how much more you, His beloved child!

"For in it [the good news] the righteousness of God is revealed from faith to faith..." (Romans 1:17) The good news is that you are the righteousness of God in Christ, which you receive from faith to faith. The just shall live by faith.

This means that this righteousness comes because you have faith in His blood, not your good behaviour, to make you right with God. It is from faith to faith, not faith to works, or works to works. The good news is not preached to show you what is wrong with you. It is preached to show you what is right with you because of Jesus' work at Calvary, despite what is wrong with you!

Additional scriptures of one being right with God through faith.

Romans 3:28 For we maintain that a man is justified by faith apart from works of the Law.

Romans 5:1 Therefore, having been justified by faith, we have peace with God through our Lord Jesus Christ,

Habakkuk 2:4 "Behold, as for the proud one, His soul is not right within him; But the righteous will live by his faith.

Romans 1:17 For in it the righteousness of God is revealed from faith to faith; as it is written, "BUT THE RIGHTEOUS man SHALL LIVE BY FAITH."

Romans 3:27 Where then is boasting? It is excluded By what kind of law? Of works? No, but by a law of faith.

Romans 4:2 For if Abraham was justified by works, he has something to boast about, but not before God.

Galatians 2:16 nevertheless knowing that a man is not justified by the works of the Law but through faith in Christ Jesus, even we have believed in Christ Jesus, so that we may be justified by faith in Christ and not by the works of the Law; since by the works of the Law no flesh will be justified.

Galatians 3:24 Therefore the Law has become our tutor to lead us to Christ, so that we may be justified by faith.

Romans 4:16 For this reason it is by faith, in order that it may be in accordance with grace, so that the promise will be guaranteed to all the descendants, not only to those who are of the Law, but also to those who are of the faith of Abraham, who is the father of us all,

HINDERANCES OF FAITH

"Unbelief." In the story of the man demon possessed son, the disciples tried to cure the boy, but instead were unsuccessful. Jesus did not say that the disciples lacked faith or did not have faith, rather that it was because of there unbelief that they could not cast out the demon. After all Jesus stated that the smallest amount of faith (a mustered seed-the smallest seed) is sufficient to remove any mountain (obstacle) if there is no unbelief present to hinder. We tend to think of faith and unbelief as opposite ends of the same pole, but according to Jesus it's possible to believe and doubt at the same time:

Jesus replied, "I tell you the truth, if you have faith *and do not doubt*, not only can you do what was done to the fig tree, but also you can say to this mountain, 'Go, throw yourself into the sea,' and it will be done." (Matt 21:21)

Of course, it's important to have faith, to believe. As Jesus said to the boy's father, "everything is possible to him who believes." But the father, like many of us, wanted God to take responsibility for the healing. "Lord, help us!" Yet Jesus said, "If *you* have faith, *you* can heal him." We think healing the sick is God's job, but He wants us to do it (Mark 16:18). Look at how the father responded:

"Lord, I believe; help my unbelief!" (Mark 9:24)

The father is saying he has faith, but he also has unbelief. **Unbelief nullifies faith** Our unbelief is cancelling our faith.

Unbelief is described in the New Testament and you will find loads of verbs or action words. Unbelief is *rejecting* Jesus (John 3:36) and *denying* the Lord (Jude 1:4). It's *thrusting away* the word of God and *judging* yourself unworthy of life (Acts 13:46). It's *suppressing* the truth (Rom 1:18) and *delighting* in wickedness (2 Th 2:12). It's *turning away* (Heb 12:25), *going astray* (2 Pet 2:15), and *trampling* the Son of God underfoot (Heb 10:29).

<u>So, If faith is a rest, then unbelief is restlessness</u>: And to whom sware he that they should not enter into his rest, but to them that believed not? So, we see that they could not enter in because of unbelief. (Heb 3:18-19, KJV)

How do we deal with unbelief? You Starve it!

And He replied to them, "This kind (of unbelief) cannot be driven out by anything but prayer and fasting." (Mk 9:29)

Unbelief that arises from ignorance and bad theology can be corrected by showing people the truth (Mk 6:6), but overcoming natural unbelief may require prayer and fasting. Your flesh needs to learn that it is not in charge – you are! By fasting for a time, you are telling your five senses that there's more to life than bread (Matt 4:4); you're saying that you prefer to live by the spirit.

Faith is expressed through love.! Gal 5:6

Questions

Question 1. Complete the following scripture. ...did not waver through regarding the promise of God but was strengthened in his faith and gave glory to God, that God had power to do what he had promised. (Rom 4:20-21)

Question 2. True or false. Faith is a work.

Question 3. True of false. Faith is a doing word.

Question 4. Does Faith Move God?

Question 5. Does Faith move you?

Question 6. How does faith come?

Question7. Give us one example of a faith in action?

Question 8 Read Gallatin's 2: 16, Romans 3:28 and Ephesians 2:8-9. How are we made right with God?

Question 9. Is it possible to be in belief and unbelief?

Question 10. What is a hinderance to faith?

Question 11. How do we access God's Grace?

Misconception regarding faith.

Mark 11:23-24 says, for assuredly, I say to you, whoever says to this mountain, 'Be removed and be cast into the sea,' and does not doubt in his heart, but believes that those things he says will be done, he will have whatever he says. ^{24}Therefore I say to you, <u>whatever things you ask</u> when you pray, believe that you receive *them,* and you will have *them.*

These verses say whatever, in the kings James version it says whatever things you desire, when you pray, believe that you receive them and you will have them. Some believer takes this to such extremes to mean they can have whatever they want. This is purely a misunderstanding of faith and lead people into having a false expectation of what is possible by faith. Ie, the winning of lottery, other people's spouses and possessions. Faith can only, yes only take what grace has already made available. Sadly, many believers don't know what has been made available through grace.

Another misconception is we have been given different levels of faith. Sadly, many translations have added to this misconception. Romans 12:3 read, For I say, through the grace given unto me, to every man that is among you, not to think *of himself* more highly than he ought to think; but to think soberly, according as God hath dealt to every man the measure of faith. (one measure). One measure. A measure of faith that never leaves us once born again.

2 Peter1:1 **Simon** Peter, a bondservant and apostle of Jesus Christ to those who have obtained like precious faith with us by the righteousness of our God and Savior Jesus Christ. The Greek word that was translated "like precious" in this verse is "isotimos," which means "of equal value or honor." We have the same faith that Peter used when he raised Dorcas from the dead (Acts 9:36-42) and when he made people whole by touching them with just his shadow (Acts 5:15).

We also have the same faith that Paul the apostle had. Paul said in Galatians 2:20, "I am crucified with Christ: nevertheless, I live; yet not I, but Christ liveth in me: and the life which I now live in the flesh I live by the faith of the Son of God, who loved me, and gave himself for me." Paul did not say that he lived by faith IN the Son of God but by the faith OF the Son of God. The measure of faith that Paul had was the same measure that Jesus had. It was Jesus' faith. If there is only one measure of faith (Rom. 12:3), then we also have the faith of Jesus.

Answers

Answers 1. 1) unbelief 2) being fully persuaded

Answers 2. False it is a rest.

Answers 3. False it is a noun (Person, place, or thing. i.e.. Jesus)

Answers 4. No. (He is not the one stuck)

Answers 5. Yes

Answers 6. By hearing and hearing the Word of Truth

Answers 7. Then man at the pool. The man with the withered hand.

Answers 8. By Grace through Faith and not works it`s a gift of God

Answers 9. Yes

Answers 10. Unbelief

Answers 11. By Faith.

———————————

"WITHOUT FAITH, GOD'S grace is wasted, & without grace, faith is powerless."

Andrew Wommack

Our greatest privilege is to know Him!

Additional reading.

"Faith arises out of being settled on God's heart and God's will for a situation - If you don't settle on who God is and His position in situations (His will for a situation), how will you ever have the realization of what you are hoping for? When will your hope ever go deeper than hope without settling the will of God in the matter? If you don't know who God is and His position for any given situation, then you are reduced to mere hope.

Faith arises from knowing God through the life of Jesus and through communion - Hope is powerful. It's the anchor of your soul. If it wasn't that it would be presumption. It would just be wishful thinking. You just want it so bad that you are presuming that you are going to get it. And you are disappointed if you don't. No, it's the evidence of what we have not yet seen. How can you have evidence of something you haven't yet seen? Because of what you have seen through faith - through your heart - through the life of Jesus - what you have seen through the secret place of knowing Him. And all of the sudden you are settled on the heart of God for a matter. And that's where the place of authority and power flows.

Faith & Disappointment

Being settled causes me not to be disappointed but drawn to know Him more - If I am clear in that place (God's heart and will for a situation), even if it seems like I lost, I can't be hurt or offended. My only moved is to know Him more because I have settled on this thing.

If I haven't settled, it's why I am so disheartened - so set back - so slapped in the face - discouraged - disappointed. Because I haven't settled on who He is in the equation, now I am subject to a whole lot of emotions, beliefs based on circumstance and not the Word and knowing Him, rather being led by feelings and lose time just trying to get through the failure of it all.

But because this perspective is so locked in even if my own spouse would pass away, it's no reflection on God whatsoever - none. If I don't know that, I am already crippled in growing in Him and knowing Him. And I have got all of this stuff going through my head and it's the way that seems right but if you look at it, it produces no life in people. It just freezes you.

Prayer of Faith

<u>Prayers from need are not prayers of faith</u>. In our language we reveal that we don't even understand, which makes all of our prayers motivated by need. It's not faith working through love. It's not even faith. It's just prayer because there is trouble. Just because we pray doesn't mean that it's faith. People pray because they are desperate, they're in trouble, they've got crisis and diagnosis, they are watching their loved ones suffer. Who's not going to pray? People that say there's no God give it a shot when they are in crisis.

The truth is if <u>One in faith it is enough</u> - Just because you have the whole world praying doesn't mean that there is faith. Sometimes it is human sentiment at best. Internet postings and prayer chains. "It's got to work out because everybody is praying."

The Bible doesn't say that the whole world has to pray. <u>One in Christ is a majority.</u> If two agree touching anything that they know is the will of God and that where we struggle (knowing the will of God). If we know it's the will of God, it will be done. So, we pray being double minded, wrong thinking nullifying faith through our unbelief.

We need to <u>Submit your experience to God's word</u>. If that's not our reality, we have a right to grow into that. If that hasn't been our experience, does that change the validity of God's word. No, we stay humble and submit our experience beneath the integrity of God's word? You can't challenge God's word with your experience. That's a mistake to judge God's word through your experience.

You judge God's word through Jesus' life.

CHAPTER SEVEN

REPENTANCE (week 7)

Repentance is a good thing! Repentance starts with Christ!

Repentance means to <u>think differently</u> (changing your mind). The Greek word commonly translated repentance (*metanoia*) literally means to <u>change your mind</u>. (You can check this out for yourself by looking up a Greek lexicon such as Thayer's and Smith's Bible Dictionary or Vines Expository Dictionary of New Testament Words.) The Greek word for repent (*metanoeo*) is similar and both words are derived from the Greek word for mind (*nous*). So, to repent is to change your mind. Nothing more, nothing less. Let's look at an example from scripture:

"The time has come," He said. "The kingdom of God is near. **Repent and believe the good news!**" (Mar 1:15)

It's more than simply trying to change the thoughts in our mind, rather, we are making an overall change in the way that thoughts get in, and what we do with them once they are in. It is not something we initiate so much as it is a response to the good news.

When Jesus said, "Repent and believe the good news" (Mk 1:15), Some might say Jesus was saying, "Stop stealing, start praying, stop cursing, start giving". Exchanging the bad content for good content. Change the Knowledge of Evil for the Knowledge of Good. But if we think different, the best we can hope for is that, once again, we can try harder. And the Gospel is not try hard but rest cause it`s done. What He was literally saying, "<u>Change the way you take in reality, see from heavens perspective, for I have come...</u>""

We don't repent to manipulate God into bringing His kingdom down; we repent because His kingdom is already at hand. (The King has come and the kingdom is within You to all that believe and receive!) We don't repent to get forgiven; we repent because we are forgiven. (He remembers your sins no more because the Cross Worked!)

As we think differently and come to walk in the revelation that Jesus is altogether lovely. That God is good all the time and He thinks we're individually His favourite, we find that the things of this world grow strangely dim. We walk away from sin effortlessly because we are captivated by something more intimate, someone more Personal and infinitely better than we could ever think Jesus!

The second part of (MK 1:15) says, "to believe the good news (Gospel)". We will take a deeper look at that in the following part.

"A curious idea men have of what repentance is! Many fancy that so many tears are to be shed, and so many groans are to be heaved, and so much despair is to be endured. Whence comes this unreasonable notion? Unbelief and despair are sins, and therefore I do not see how they can be constituent elements of acceptable repentance; yet there are many who regard them as necessary parts of true Christian experience. They are in great error ... To repent is to change your mind (think differently) about sin, and Christ, and all the great things of God." Charles Spurgoen

In Luke 24:47 we read,

"And that repentance and remission of sins should be preached in his name among all nations, beginning at Jerusalem." KJV

"It was also written that this message would be proclaimed in the authority of his name to all the nations, beginning in Jerusalem: 'There is forgiveness of sins for all who repent." NLT

In Luke 24 - Jesus was raised from the dead and said that the Christ should suffer this way at the hands of the gentiles so that repentance and remission (forgiveness) of sin would be preached to all nations. The purpose of His suffering and raising from the dead was that repentance - change mind would lead to a change in direction - and forgiveness of sin would be preached to all nations.

If God can change the way, we think He can change the way we live. If God can change our perspective through truth, He can change our lives. The Gospel (good news) opens up a door for you to think differently so you can live differently.

Repentance is not perfection. In the parable of the prodigal son a clear picture of the Gospel is portrait for us. How the very goodness of the Father led to repentance and restoration of a son.

Let's read, Luke together 15:13-24 "Not long after that, the younger son got together all he had, set off for a distant country and there squandered his wealth in wild living. After he had spent everything, there was a severe famine in that whole country, and he began to be in need. So, he went and hired himself out to a citizen of that country, who sent him to his fields to feed pigs.He longed to fill his stomach with the pods that the pigs were eating, but no one gave him anything. "When he came to his senses, he said, 'How many of my father's hired servants have food to spare, and here I am starving to death! I will set out and go back to my father and say to him: Father, I have sinned against heaven and against you. I am no longer worthy to be called your son; make me like one of your hired servants.' So, he got up and went to his father. "But while he was still a long way off, his father saw him and was filled with compassion for him; he ran to his son, threw his arms around him and kissed him. "The son said to him, 'Father, I have sinned against heaven and against you.

I am no longer worthy to be called your son.' "But the father said to his servants, 'Quick! Bring the best robe and put it on him. Put a ring on his finger and sandals on his feet. Bring the fattened calf and kill it. Let's have a feast and celebrate. For this son of mine was dead and is alive again; he was lost and is found.' So, they began to celebrate.

WOW, that just awesome. In Luke 15:11-12 Jesus said "And he said, A certain man has two sons: And the younger of them said to his Father, Father, give me the portion of goods that falleth to me. And he divided unto them his living." The younger son wanted his inheritance before his father died, which is quite unusual, but his father granted the request and gave his sons their inheritance. Verse 13 Says, "And not many days after the younger son gathered all together, and took his journey into a far country, and there wasted his substance with riotous living." The younger son took all of his wealth, his part of the inheritance, went into a distant country, and wasted it in riotous living. One translation says, "Partying and spending money on prostitutes." Verses 14-15 read, "And when he has spent all, there arose a mighty famine in that land (The land became destitute, and people were starving); and he began to be in want. And he wanted and joined himself to a citizen of that country; and he sent him into his fields to feed swine" (brackets mine). He got a Job working for a man in that country and he was sent to feed the pigs.

VERSE 16 SAYS, "AND he would fain have filled his belly with the husks of that the swine did eat: and no man gave unto him." He was so hungry, at the point of starvation, and he said, "Just give me the pigs food - anything," but no one gave him anything. He had squandered all of his inheritance. Verse 17 continues, "And when he came to himself, he said, how many hired servants have my father's bread enough to spare, and I perish with hunger!" One translation says," When he came to his senses." In other words, his father's servants had more than enough food, and he was dying of hunger.

He made a decision: <u>he repented</u>. In verses 18-19, he said: "I will arise and go to my father, and say unto him, Father, I have sinned against heaven, and before thee, and am no more worthy to be called son: make me as one of thy hired servants." "Just make me a slave, Father. I've sinned against you, squandered your living, and sinned against God. Just make me a slave." then he arose and went to his father. Repentance is more than just a change of attitude, it leads a person to act on what they believe, to turn around or (or return) and go in a new direction. We've all turned away from God, Our Father, and from heaven our home. The Bible says Isaiah 53:6 that "tall we like sheep has gone astray: we have turned everyone to his own way" but God in His mercy took our sins and laid them on Jesus. The story continues in verses 20-24. "And he arose and came to his father." "Son, look what you've done. You've wasted all my wealth; all I accumulated in my life. Be one of my slaves."

Most earthly fathers would probably be very angry and have an attitude like that but notice the attitude of this father: "But when he was yet a great way off, his father saw him and had compassion (love came out of his heart for his son), and ran, and fell on his neck, and kissed him. And the son said unto him, Father I have sinned against heaven, and in thy sight, and am no more worthy to be called thy son. But the father said to his servants, "Bring forth the best robe and put it on him; and put a ring on his hand, and shoes on his feet: and bring hither the fatted calf, and kill it; let us eat, and be merry: For this my son was dead, and is alive again; he was lost, and is found. And they began to celebrate".

Hearing the Gospel is in essence bring you to repentance. And repentance becomes a way of living!

Questions

Question 1. What does Repentance mean?

Question 2. Read Romans 2:4 What leads one to repentance?

Question 3. Read Isaiah 55:7. What must the wicked do?

Question 4. What two things must the unrighteous do?

Question 5. What will God do for the person who does those things stated above?

Question 6. Read 2 Peter 3:9. What is God's desire for all people?

Question 7. In the Story of the prodigal son who represent the son?

Question 8. In the story of the prodigal son who represents the Father?

Question 9. Complete the following statement. For my was and is a again; he was , and now is .

Question 10. What is repentance not? 1) 2) .

Answers

1. To think differently (change one mind, God did the change of Heart, you Chose the change of direction)
2. The goodness of God.
3. Forsake their ways.
4. Forsake their thoughts and return to the Lord.
5. Have mercy and pardon abundantly.
6. To Repent
7. We do
8. Out Heavenly Father
9. Son. Dead. Alive. Lost. Found
10. 1. Crying and wailing. 2. Perfection and behaviour modification.

A WRONG CONCEPT ABOUT REPENTANCE?

1. Repentance is not that you must weep and wail when you repent. But you need to show some godly sorrow. "Repentance must be marked by regret, tears, and grief-stricken anguish. 2 Cor 7:10 reads "Godly sorrow brings repentance that leads to salvation and leaves no regret, but worldly sorrow brings death." Godly sorrow is not something you have to manufacture to impress the Lord. Nor is it a work that has to accompany your faith. Godly sorrow is when God works through the aches and hurts of our mistakes to draw us to himself. If your sorrow leads you to God, then it's good and godly sorrow. But if it leads you away from him, perhaps because you have been told to focus on your unworthiness, then it's not. Now I'm glad – not that you were upset, but that you were jarred into turning things around. You let the distress bring you to God, not drive you from him. The result was all gain, no loss. Distress that drives us to God does that. It turns us around. It gets us back in the way of salvation. We never regret that kind of pain. But those who let distress drive them away from God are full of regrets, end up on a deathbed of regrets. (2 Cor 7:9-10, MSG)

IT DOESN'T JUST MEAN to say, "I'm sorry." That can be regret or condemnation – "Oh woe is me". Just because you said it or feel it, It doesn't mean that there has been a change of mind and direction. And what gives us the hope and the inspiration to think differently is understanding the forgiveness of sin. That God's not holding our trespasses against us. Because that is what makes you hopeless.

Don't ever fall for the lie that says, "repentance without tears is meaningless worthless." When you encounter the goodness of God in an unexpected way, the important thing is not whether you laugh or cry but that you repent – that you embrace what God is showing you and allow his grace to change you!

1. The root of repentance is behaviour modification (a change of behaviour). No, behaviour change is the fruit or result of a changed

philosophy (way of thinking differently).

Let me explain.

When we study the word "philosophy" and put it into a biblical context it refers to the traditions, ideas and values from the world, which is ruled by the devil which are oppose to God's values and how the kingdom of heaven operates. We should guard against letting the devil rob us of what God has already given us, namely, all the things we need to live a godly life. He convinces us to put worldly traditions over God's truths, and twists what the Scriptures actually say into a completely different message. Such as the concept of repentance.

The philosophy we accept has everything to do with what enters our mind, and what is in our mind eventually enters into our heart. (ref. Colossians 2:8)

Real repentance is not just a change in behaviour. It comes from inside, and it is triggered by a change of heart (what you believe). Repentance and belief are on the same side of the same coin. You can't have one without the other. So, to have a change of heart, we must have a change in the way of thinking first. We need to believe with our heart, and then verbally give voice to what is in our heart (ref. Romans 10:10).

The thoughts we have in our mind determine what is in our heart. This, in turn, determines our actions and who we are (ref. Proverbs 23:7). What is in our heart affects our entire life. Therefore, we must be careful what we let enter into it (ref. Proverbs 4:23). Through what lens do we read the Word. Is it through our degrees, our culture, our traditions or our preconceived ideas?

The devil has blinded the minds of those who do not believe the Gospel (good news), so that they cannot be transform or renew the way the Scriptures instruct us (2 Corinthians 4:4). We must first change our way of thinking and think differently, which is the first step to seeking true repentance (Romans 12:1, 2, *AMP*).

<u>Renewing the mind to His way of doing is a continuous lifetime process!</u>

IT`S ABOUT HEART TRANSFORMATION not behaviour modification for right believing will result in right doing effortless!

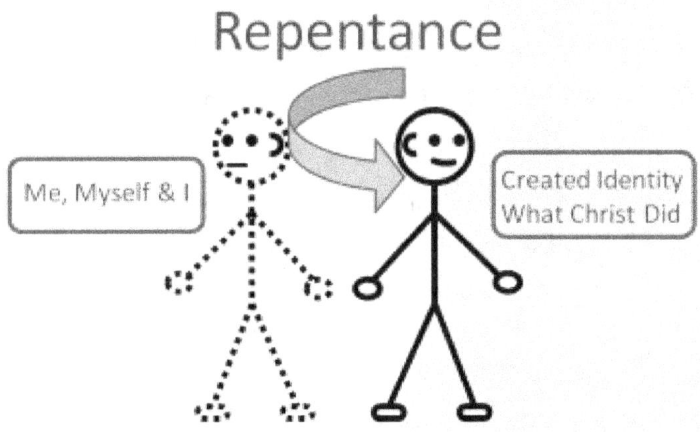

CHAPTER EIGHT

Church (week 8)

The Greek word for "church" is ecclesia and literally means an assembly of people together for the purpose of worship or prayer or praise or just looking unto God.

I'm going to read some other things here. It says, "Ecclesia in the New Testament can encompass any number of believers. It can be used of small groups that met in homes (Romans 16:5). It encompassed all believers living in a large city (Acts 11:22), or a large geographical district, such as Asia or Galatia." It goes on to say, "The typical meeting of the church was in a home. When such a congregation met 'everyone [had] a hymn, a word of instruction, a revelation, a tongue or an interpretation' (1 Corinthians 14:26). Individuals shared and others 'weighed carefully what was said' (1 Corinthians 14:29) ...such sharing remains essential to the very existence of the church as a community of faith...Each person was expected to contribute and to serve others with his or her spiritual gift(s)."

Chances are, you've heard someone say, "I love God, but I don't have to go to church to prove it." They're right! Jesus does not say, "And this is how you know that you love me—if you attend church." We saints are the Church.

If going to church is not required to show our love for God, what is the point of church?

The answer may surprise you. Part of your growth in Christ only happens when being in community with other believers. It is the equivalent of trying to become a great soccer player alone. There is only so much you can learn on your own; after a while you need to be on a team to really understand the sport and hone your skills.

Christianity is a team sport. We can definitely learn truths alone; however, these truths are fleshed out in community with other believers. As you learned on day four, part of being a disciple is uniting with other believers. If you want to be all God created you to be, it happens in biblical community.

Attending Weekly worship services contribute to our growth in multiple ways.

1. **It's a place to connect with other believers. (fellowship)**

"All...who had believed were together and had all things in common; and they began selling their property and possessions and were sharing them with all, as anyone might have need. Day by day continuing with one mind in the temple, breaking bread from house to house, they were taking their meals together with gladness and sincerity of heart..." (Acts 2:44–46)

Why should I attend church?

2. **It's a place to worship God.**

"Praise the Lord! Praise God in his sanctuary; praise him in his mighty heaven!" (Psalm 150:1)

We come to worship the ONE, the great I AM. Yes, we do this at home, in the car anywhere but there is something for collective praise and worship of our God, Lord and King.

3. **It's a place to hear Scripture taught.**

"All the believers devoted themselves to the apostles' teaching..." (Acts 2:42).

Where we can receive revelation from God. Have you possibly been in a service with a partner and you both received got two different messaged from the sermon. Its because God spoke directly to what you need.

4. **It's a place to serve others.**

"God has given each of you a gift from his great variety of spiritual gifts. Use them well to serve one another" (1 Peter 4:10).

5. **It's a place to find encouragement.**

"And let us not neglect our meeting together, as some people do, but encourage one another, especially now that the day of his return is drawing near" (Hebrews 10:25).

---

6. **It's a place to be challenged.**

"As iron sharpens iron, so one man sharpens another" (Proverbs 27:17).

The Relationship

In Ephesians 4, Paul shares how each person in the body of Christ is important and needed. "As each part does its own special work, it helps the other parts grow, so that the whole body is healthy and growing and full of love" (Ephesians 4:16 NLT). Each Christian has something to contribute to the church. When we are willing to get involved, serve, and work together— "the whole body is healthy and growing and full of love."

When speaking to believers in Corinth, Paul tells them that they are dependent upon each other. "The way God designed our bodies is a model for understanding our lives together as a church: every part dependent on every other part" (1 Corinthians 12:25). It's not only nice to be with other believers; it's necessary. We need each other. Part of our growth in Christ only happens when being in community with other believers. The Key is that we live from His life.

How do you find a group of believers that's right for you?

• Pray for discernment and leading.

• Look for a church that faithfully teaches God's Word, Grace and not mixture of covenants.

• Find a church that is serious about revealing your new identity as sons and daughters of God (Grace based disciples).

• Get involved.

• If it fits—stay; if it doesn't fit—find a church that does.

<u>Why is it important to assemble with other believers?</u>

Part of your growth in Christ only happens in community.

Christianity is a team sport not a spectator sport. It is a collective pursuit. If you want to be all God created you to be, it only happens in biblical community.

Biblical community is more than showing up to church on Sunday. It's more than attending a Bible study or grabbing a meal with another Christian. It's about uniting our lives together around a common goal, pursuing a common purpose, and living together as citizens of Christ's kingdom.

When the twelve disciples were called to follow Christ, they were not called individually for a one-year internship program, good as that maybe.

They were called collectively for a lifelong journey.

• **They were together in pursuit**: When Jesus taught, the disciples were together with Him (Matt 5:1–7:29). When Jesus ministered, the disciples were together with Him. When Jesus performed miracles, the disciples were together with Him (Matt 8:23–27).

• **They were together in service**: When Jesus feed the 5,000 and the 4,000, the disciples served the people together. When Jesus sent out the twelve and later send out the 70, He sent them two by two (Mark 6:7–13; Luke 10:1–16). They served together.

• **They were together with questions**: They didn't understand the hard sayings of Christ (Mark 8). They had questions about Christ's identity (Matt 8:27). They didn't always understand His miracles.

• **They were together in love.** In John 13:35–36, Jesus said, "A new commandment I give to you, that you love one another even as I have loved you, that you also love one another. By this all men will know that you are My disciples, if you have love for one another."

• **They were together in encouragement.** In Luke 22:31, Jesus said to Simon Peter, "Satan has demanded permission to sift you like wheat; but I have prayed for you, that your faith may not fail; and you, when once you have turned again, strengthen your brothers."

• **They were together in mission.** Jesus told the disciples in Matt 28:19–20, "Go therefore and make disciples of all the nations, baptizing them in the name of the Father and Son and the Holy Spirit, teaching them to observe all that I commanded you...".

The disciples were together in their pursuit of Christ, together in their service for Christ, together in their questions about Christ, together in their learning and love for each other, together in their encouragement, together in mission. They travelled together, ate together, and ministered together. Their lives were intentionally woven together.

The atmosphere created by Christ was not a competition. He created an environment where community aided in growth. They weren't alone. They didn't have to figure it all out by themselves. They were securely placed in a community that offered encouragement, strength, accountability, belonging, friendship, and various gifts.

Enter your local church information below.

<u>About Our Church</u> (Enter your church details below)

What we Believe

Our History

Our Leadership

Our Vision

Our Contact details

Our Contact details

CHAPTER NINE

Water Baptism

Jesus commanded that believers be baptized (Mark 16:16; Matthew 28:19).

The English word "baptize" is transliterated from a Greek word, "baptidzo", which simply means "to dip, to overwhelm, to plunge, to submerge." It more accurately means "to cause something to be dipped or beneath the surface of water or some other fluid." It is also a verb, meaning an action, state, or occurrence, and forming the main part of the predicate of a sentence, such as *hear, become, happen.*

If this word was truly translated, rather than transliterated, the command in the New Testament would read "Go therefore and make disciples of all the nations, fully submerge them in the name of the Father and of the Son and of the Holy Spirit" (Matthew 28:19).

Many believe that water baptism is a part of salvation but in truth it is placing faith in understanding the redemptive work of Christ that produces salvation – not actions. Grace alone does not save. Faith alone does not save. But it's the combination of grace and faith and both are a free gift from God, Eph 2:8-9 but saving faith has actions. (James 2:20) and the action is water baptism in the context baptism. Baptism represents the death, burial and resurrection of Jesus. The believer, by faith, steps into an outward sign of an inward grace. You are saying that you are dying in the likeness of His death.

Being baptised does not make you more saved and is not a requirement for salvation. You don't score extra bonus brownie points.

Water baptism is a command of Jesus and is the initial anchor upon believe meaning that when one looks to scripture one sees that water baptism always followed the believing believer. Water baptism carries such a significance because of the grace that comes on you. But it`s more than doing it because Jesus said so. It` out of knowing Him, relationship.

In Him you were also circumcised with the circumcision made without hands, by putting off the body of the sins of the flesh, by the circumcision of Christ, buried with Him in baptism, in which you also were raised with Him through faith in the working of God, who raised Him from the dead. Colossians 2:11-12

In Acts chapter 8 we read the story of Philip and the Eunuch we see Preaching Jesus included water baptism, v.35-36 - Then Philip opened his mouth, and began at the same scripture, and preached unto him Jesus. And as they went on *their* way, they came unto a certain water: and the eunuch said, See, *here is* water; what doth hinder me to be baptized? - Water baptism was a part of preaching Jesus to the eunuch. It must have been a highlight of the message. Philip didn't preach Jesus apart from water baptism. He didn't preach about a prayer to go to heaven. He was preaching death, burial and resurrection. He was preaching: Say goodbye to the old man. Say hello to the new. Repent (think differently) and rise up and live in the nature of God because the kingdom is here.

There are several scriptures of those that are saved and filled with the Holy Spirit being baptised in water after being born again and receiving the baptism of the Holy Spirit. When you understand it`s meaning, which is that You died with Christ and You were also raised in Christ).

- Acts 10:44-48 While Peter was still speaking these words, the Holy Spirit fell upon all those who were listening to the message. All the circumcised believers who came with Peter were amazed, because the gift of the Holy Spirit had been poured out on the Gentiles also. For they were hearing them speaking with tongues and exalting God. Then Peter answered, "Surely no one can refuse the water for these to be baptised who have received the Holy Spirit just as we *did*, can he?" And he ordered them to be baptised in the name of Jesus Christ. Then they asked him to stay on for a few days.

• Acts 19:1-7 It happened that while Apollos was at Corinth, Paul passed through the upper country and came to Ephesus, and found some disciples. He said to them, "Did you receive the Holy Spirit when you believed?" And they *said* to him, "No, we have not even heard whether there is a Holy Spirit (the second born-again experience)." And he said, "Into what then were you baptised?" And they said, "Into John's baptism (water baptism)." Paul said, "John baptised with the baptism of repentance, telling the people to believe in Him who was coming after him, that is, in Jesus." When they heard this, they were baptised (of the Spirit) in the name of the Lord Jesus. And when Paul had laid his hands upon them, the Holy Spirit came on them, and they *began* peaking with tongues and prophesying. There were in all about twelve men.

"Water baptism has everything to do with newness of life - the transformation of life and the resurrection power of God."

Dan Mohler Sr

In the Old Testament, God gave a covenant to Abraham in which He required those who were participating in the covenant to accept and experience the sign and seal of the covenant which was a natural circumcision of the flesh (Genesis 17:10-14).

Today water baptism is a sign of the new covenant in the same way circumcision was in the old covenant. Post Cross it is an outwards expression of an inward change. <u>It's about understanding transformation not salvation.</u>

In Him you were also circumcised with the circumcision made without hands, by putting off the body of the sins of the flesh, by the circumcision of Christ, buried with Him in baptism, in which you also were raised with Him through faith in the working of God, who raised Him from the dead. Colossians 2:11-12

What, then, shall we say? shall we continue in the sin (noun) that the grace may abound? let it not be! we who died to the sin (noun) — how shall we still live in it? are ye ignorant that we, as many as were baptized to Christ Jesus, to his death were baptised? we were buried together, then, with him through the baptism to the death, that even as Christ was raised up out of the dead through the glory of the Father, so also we in newness of life might walk.

For, if we have become planted together to the likeness of his death, [so] also we shall be of the rising again; this knowing, that our old man was crucified with [him], that the body of the sin (noun) may be made useless, for our no longer serving the sin (noun); for he who hath died hath been set free from the sin. Romans 6:1-6

"Baptism does have requirements." The first and most important requirement is being born again. He who believes and is baptized will be saved; but he who does not believe will be condemned. Mark 16:16. Believing come first.

The second must be old enough to know (understanding why) what they are doing. (Acts 8:12; 10:47). So, an infant can't be biblical baptised. Parents dedicate their infants to the Lord. So, when one believes, and understands the reason ie, that we died and were resurrected in Christ then one is privileged to be water baptised. (Rom 6)

"Misconceptions of water baptism." Being baptised merely because one wants to become part of a church group. There is no scriptural reference for this.

Another is that water baptism removes our sins. Now when they heard this, they were cut to the heart, and said to Peter and the rest of the apostles, "Men and brethren, what shall we do?" Then Peter said to them, "Repent, and let every one of you be baptized in the name of Jesus Christ **for** the remission of sins; and you shall receive the gift of the Holy Spirit. Acts 2:37-38.

The "for" in Acts 2:37-38 is communicating the fact that they were to be baptised "as the result of" or "because of" already had believed and in doing so had already received forgiveness of their sins when taken in light of other scripture.

In fact, according to the law of Moses, nearly everything was purified with blood. For without the shedding of blood, there is no forgiveness. Hebrews 9:22

In him we have redemption through his blood, the forgiveness of sins, in accordance with the riches of God's grace. Ephesian 1:7

Not to mention this interpretation of the passage in Acts 2:37-38 is also consistent with the message recorded in Peter's next two sermons to unbelievers where he associates the forgiveness of sins with the act of repentance and faith in Christ without even mentioning baptism (Acts 3:17-26; Acts 4:8-12).

QUESTION

Question 1. Read Acts 10:43, salvation comes to us how?

Question 2. Baptism is an expression of faith that usually takes place at the time of salvation. How does Acts 2:38 express this truth?

Question 3. How does Mark 16:16 express this truth?

Question 4. Baptism is a way of calling upon the Lord. How does Acts 22:16 express this truth?

Question 5. True of False that Water Baptism is a way to call upon the Lord for a clear conscience?

Question 6. What is the requirement for baptism, according to Acts 2:38?

Question 7. What is the requirement for baptism, according to Mark 16:16?

Question 8. Can an infant believe or repent?

Question 9. True or False. Water baptism is about understanding salvation not transformation.

Question 10. Complete the following statement. In him we have , the forgiveness of sins, in accordance with . Ephesian 1:7

Additional reading

This is He who came by water and blood—Jesus Christ; not only by water, but by water and blood. And it is the Spirit who bears witness, because the Spirit is truth. For there are three that bear witness in heaven: the Father, the Word, and the Holy Spirit; and these three are one. And there are three that bear witness on earth: the Spirit, the water, and the blood; and these three agree as one. 1 John 5:6-8 NLT

Answers

Answer 1. Freely, as a gift through faith in Jesus.

Answer 2. Peter said "repent and be baptised."

Answer 3. Jesus said, "he that believes and is baptised shall be saved." Implying that it can happen at the same time.

Answer 4. The Scripture says that a person calls upon the name of the Lord, there sins will be washed away, It appears that calling on the name of the Lord can be vocal or through the act of baptism, as it appears in this scripture.

Answer 5. True

Answer 6. Repentance

Answer 7. A person must believe.

Answer 8. No

Answer 9. False

Answer 10. Redemption through His blood, the riches of His Grace.

CHAPTER TEN

THE BAPTISM OF THE Holy Spirit

Before we get into studying the Baptism of the Holy Spirit it`s vital to know who the Holy Spirit is. Gaining an understanding of who the Holy Spirit is, and who He is not, is critical in order to experience His presence and power. The Holy Spirit is not, a dove, a wind, tongues of fire, a feeling, or an emotion. Although His presence can stir up emotions within you, and is as gentle as a dove etc, He is the third person of the Trinity God the Father, God the Son and God the Holy Spirit. When you receive Jesus Christ as your Lord and Saviour, the Holy Spirit comes to live in your heart; it becomes His dwelling place.

<u>The Christian life is an impossibility without Him</u>!

You can cultivate your relationship with the Holy Spirit by praising God, reading the Word, praying, and singing spiritual songs (see ref. Ephesians 5:19). Doing these things helps to edifies your spirit and makes you more sensitive to His presence. Invite Him into every situation and atmosphere in which you find yourself. When you acknowledge Him this way, He will be able to move in your life. The Holy Spirit and the Word is predominantly the voice we hear today in Christ.

Howbeit when he, the Spirit of truth, is come, he will guide you into all truth: for he shall not speak of himself; but whatsoever he shall hear, *that* shall he speak: and he will show you things to come. John 16:13.

He speaks on behalf of both the Father and the Son. Jesus said that Holy Spirit doesn't speak on His own but what He hears. He is directly communicating the Father's heart and wisdom to us His beloved. The person of Holy Spirit is with us and in us.

And I will ask the Father, and He will give you another Comforter (Counsellor, Helper, Intercessor, Advocate, Strengthener, and Standby), that He may remain with you forever. (John 14:26) AMPC

After the resurrection Jesus told His disciples to wait for the promise of the Father, the Holy Spirit. (see ref. Acts 1:4-5) Jesus did not want the disciple trying to advance the kingdom in their own strength. In Acts 1:8 we read, "But you will receive **power** when the Holy Spirit comes upon you. And you will be my witnesses, telling people about me everywhere—in Jerusalem, throughout Judea, in Samaria, and to the ends of the earth." The Word power here is "Dunamis" meaning miraculous pawer, ability and might. It was this very power that worked through Jesus (see Acts 10:38). Yes, we have the same Holy Spirit that raised Christ from the dead (see ref. Rom 8:11) and we can be expectant to see miraculous in and through our lives, if we will believe. (see ref. John 14:12). In Act 2:1-6 The promise became the reality.

The Holy Spirit is the best Friend we always dreamed of!

The work of the Holy Spirit.

And when He comes, He will convict *and* convince the world *and* bring demonstration (guilt) to it about sin and about righteousness (uprightness of heart and right standing with God) and about judgment:

⁹About sin, because they do not believe in Me [trust in, rely on, and adhere to Me];

¹⁰About righteousness (uprightness of heart and right standing with God), because I go to My Father, and you will see Me no longer;

¹¹About judgment, because the ruler (evil genius, prince) of this world [Satan] is judged *and* condemned *and* sentence already is passed upon him. John 16:8-11

When he comes, he will prove that the world's people *are guilty*. (John 16:8 NIrV)

The word guilt is not in the original Greek. It was added in the 1970s by translators working for the International Bible Society. It is the ministry of the Holy Spirit to reprove of sin, righteousness, and judgement. It's not our ministry to be judge or jury. We are simply a witness testifying to the wonderous and marvellous good news of the Gospel.

So how does the Holy Spirit convict (convinces) us? He does it by turning on the lights, not to shame you (Jesus carried your shame), but to our unbelief (our lack of trust in the finished work of the Cross). He does not remind us of our sins (Heb 8:12 and Heb 10:17) but show us the way to life reminding us the believer, that we have been made right with God and to the unbeliever there need for Jesus. We know this because it`s a singular sin (noun) John 16:9 that of unbelief. This is the only sin that send one to hell and is the unpardonable sin. Rejecting Jesus.

What is the difference between being born again and the baptism of the Holy Spirit?

We see in the book of Acts separate experiences from that of being born again. In one instance, Philp was preaching in the city of Samaria, and the entire city believed. (see ref. Acts 8:4-8) During that time Philp performed many miracles, but then we read the following in Acts 8:14-17 "Now when the apostles in Jerusalem heard that Samaria had received the word of God, they sent them Peter and John, who came down and prayed for them that they might receive the Holy Spirit. For He had not yet fallen upon any of them; they had simply been baptized [in the name of the Lord Jesus. Then they *began* laying their hands on them, and they were receiving the Holy Spirit.

Again, we see another example of a second born again experience this time with Paul the Apostle in Acts 19:1-7 It happened that while Apollos was at Corinth, Paul passed through the upper country and came to Ephesus, and found some disciples. He said to them, "Did you receive the Holy Spirit when you believed?" And they *said* to him, "No, we have not even heard whether there is a Holy Spirit."And he said, "Into what then were you baptized?" And they said, "Into John's baptism." Paul said, "John baptized with the baptism of repentance, telling the people to believe in Him who was coming after him, that is, in Jesus." When they heard this, they were baptized in the name of the Lord Jesus. And when Paul had laid his hands upon them, the Holy Spirit came on them, and they *began* speaking with tongues and prophesying. There were in all about twelve men.

It`s pretty clear that there are two different events in scripture after the day of Pentecost. One of being born again and the other the baptism of the Holy Spirit. In essence it`s the Holy Spirit that baptises us in the Body of Christ and at baptism its Christ who baptise us into the Holy Spirit.

<u>You might be thinking but wait did I get all of the Holy Spirits ability when I received Jesus being born again?</u> You get the Holy Spirit when you are born again, because you can't have the Spirit of God in you to be born again (see ref. 1 Cor. 12:13. You are sealed by the Holy spirit, approved and enclosed becoming the temple of the Holy Spirit. (1 Cor 6:19) So, if you don't speak in tongues or prophesy you are not any less saved, than those that do. There is so much more to experience simply being born again. We have to cooperate with the Holy Spirit for He will never force Himself on anyone. He is the perfect gentleman. You don't have to be baptized in the Holy Spirit; you get to.

At the new birth our nature changes. At the baptism in the Holy Spirit our ability changes.

The baptism of the Holy Spirit is simply an act of recognizing, acknowledging, and welcoming the Holy Spirit and His work, power, ability, and presence in your life.

Tongues. Speaking in tongues is still valid and I would go as far as saying a necessity in a Christian wanting to live the victories life. Speaking in tongues is a grace gift, a manifestation of the Holy Spirits power in us after we have received the baptism of the Holy Spirit.

It is when the Holy Spirit inspire our spirit to pray to God, using the same vocal cords we use to speak. Making sounds our natural minds can't comprehend. (see ref. 1 Cor. 14:2). We see in every instance that when the Baptism of the Holy spirit was received there was evidence of speaking in tongues. Every time.

But why should I speak in tongues? Am I not going to be like a puppet and the Holy Spirit the puppet Master? Speaking in tongues built your faith (see ref. Jude 20). It also helps to draw out into your natural mind the wisdom that is in your Born-Again spirit man which just like Jesus. Your Spirit Man contains the mind of Christ (see ref. 1 Cor 2:16) and knows all things (see ref. 1 John 2:20) and speaking in tongues draws it out. Speaking in tongues also brings a supernatural rest and refreshing. (see ref. Is. 28:11-12) and will enable us to give thanks to God way above our natural limits our natural tongue. (see ref. 1 Cor 14:15-17).

Hinderance to speaking in tongues. One hinderance is simply a lack of knowledge (revelation) and another is simply unbelief. If God who is good how would not any gift from Him not be good. Sadly, many have been taught wrongly regarding tongues and in that have replace a lie with truth. As stated earlier not speaking in tongues does not mean you are not saved or that you will instantly speak in the tongue of angels when you received the baptism of the Holy Spirit. I received the baptism of the Holy Spirit but only spoke in tongues several months later due to a renewing of the mind and replacing the lie with truth.

How long should I pray in the Spirit? Its about knowing Him. Do you say to you loved one how much time do I need to spend with you today? An hour, two maybe 5. No, we are always in the Spirit even when we don't speak in tongues. Yes, its important to spend time, as Paul the Apostle stated in 1 Cor 14:18, "I thank God that I speak in tongues more than all of you."

And we know from the context of Chapter 14 that he was referring to speaking in the tongues of angels. (see. Ref 1 Cor 14:2).

How does speaking in tongues work? Just as with salvation God does not make you receive. He isn't going to make you speak I tongue. God does not take over peoples' bodies. Its not a shot gun wedding. You can't just open your mouth and wait for a sound to come out. As you begin to utter words the Holy Spirit is inspiring you to speak, the words will come out more and more easily. You won't understand and it will sound like nonsense but keep at it. The natural mind can't understand what is spiritual (see ref. 1 Cor 2:14) but one can ask for an interpretation (see ref 1 Cor 14:13). Getting an interpretation does not mean a word of word translation, it could be that in the future God will give you a word of knowledge or wisdom. The only time an interpretation is required immediate is during a church service. It is not necessary when praying in privately.

A Quick note on the Gifts of the Spirit - Gifts flow out of knowing Him. They are encompassed by the person of Holy Spirit. He has every one of the gifts. Is it right to desire spiritual gifts you might be asking yourself? Absolutely. Are we chasing after gifts? No. They are in Him - they are who He is. And we are in Him so every spiritual gift is already in us for we have been blessed with every spiritual gift (see ref. Eph 1:3 and 1 Cor 1:7). There are 9 gifts. 1. The Word of Knowledge 2. The Word of Wisdom 3. The Gift of Prophecy 4. The Gift of Faith 5. The Gifts of Healings 6. The Working of Miracles 7. The Discerning of Spirits 8. Different Kinds of Tongues 9. The Interpretation of Tongues

A quick note on the fruit on the spirit. In Gal 5:22-23 we read the following

But the Holy Spirit produces this kind of fruit in our lives: love, joy, peace, patience, kindness, goodness, faithfulness, [23]gentleness, and self-control.

An important key is that it is a singular fruit (**one**) of the spirit yet multifunction in operation and functionality. Not something we need to master but to live out from within.

Questions

Question 1. Who is the Holy Spirit?

Question 2. On whose behalf does the Holy Spirit speak on?

Question 3. Name two benefits of speaking in a heavenly Tongues

1)

2)

Question 4. What does the Holy Spirit convince the unbeliever of?

Question 5. What does the Holy Spirit convince the believer of?

Question 6. True of False. The baptism of the Holy Spirit is still valid for today?

Question 7. Name one hinderance to receiving the baptism of the Holy Spirit?

Question 8. What is the only requirement to receive the baptism of the Holy Spirit?

Question 9. Name two gifts of the Spirit?

1)

2)

Question 10. How many fruits of the Holy Spirit are there?

How do we receive the Baptism of the Holy Spirit?

There is only one requirement to receiving the baptism of the Holy Spirit. You need to be born again. Jesus does all the work. In the same way you believed when Jesus came to live in you. You simply believed the Good News and gave voice to your declaration of belief.

He is the one that baptises you into the Holy Spirit (see ref. Matt 3:11), so if you have not it would be our great pleasure to do so.

Let us all pray this together believing in our hearts for this incredible grace gift that will empower us to life the victorious Christian life.

"Father, I thank you that I am the Temple of the Holy Spirit, I welcome You to fill me right now. Thank You for filling me with your presence. Amen"

Answers

Answer 1. God the Spirit. The third person of the Triune God. One God three persons.

Answer 2. The Father and the Son.

Answer 3. Supernatural rest. Draws out the wisdom of God. Builds you up. Empowers you from within.

Answer 4. Unbelief

Answer 5. Right standing (righteousness)

Answer 6. True.

Answer 7. Unbelief. Wrong teaching. Fear.

Answer 8. To be born again.

Answer 9. 1. The Word of Knowledge 2. The Word of Wisdom 3. The Gift of Prophecy 4. The Gift of Faith 5. The Gifts of Healings 6. The Working of Miracles 7. The Discerning of Spirits 8. Different Kinds of Tongues 9. The Interpretation of Tongues

Answer 10. is a singular fruit (**one**) of the spirit yet multifunction in operation and functionality.

"Oh, my friends, I would fain repeat it to you a hundred times—*The Spirit of God within me is a Person*! I am only an earthen vessel, but in that earthen vessel I carry a treasure of unspeakable worth..."

Watchman Nee (*The Normal Christian Life*)

CHAPTER ELEVEN

Entering God's Rest

With billions spent on getaways, holidays and spa`s but still the vast majority come back needing a holiday from their holiday. True rest is found in a person. The promised sabbath rest if found not in observations to keeping the requirements of sabbath keeping. According to the Jewish faith to keep the Sabbath holy, which means that Jews were not supposed to work on Saturdays. But to clarify this, the Jewish scholars created 39 separate categories of what "work" means, and within those 39 categories there are many sub-categories. So, to follow the rule of not working on the Sabbath (which is one aspect), there are literally thousands of sub-rules to follow, including how many steps you can take (no more than 2000 for the day), and how many letters you can write on the Sabbath. Day.

In the book of Hebrews written primarily to the Hebrews the anonymous author reminds us that there remains, then, a Sabbath-rest for the people of God; for anyone who enters God's rest also rests from his own work, just as God did from his. Hebrews 4:9-10

The Sabbath is not Sunday and has never been contrary to some denominational ideologies.

The Sabbath was first mentioned in Scripture in Exodus 16, when the Lord started miraculously providing the children of Israel with manna in the wilderness. Shortly after this, the Lord commanded the observance of the Sabbath day in the ten commandments that were communicated to Moses on Mt. Sinai on the two tablets of stone (Ex. 20:8-11). In this command, God connected this Sabbath day with the rest that He took on the seventh day of creation. This rest was not because God was tired but because He was finished. Think of it this way, just as a painter completes his mater piece knowing that adding even one more brush stroke will ruin the masterpiece, so to was it with God. His creation was prefect, so He rested.

Deuteronomy 5:15, also clearly states that the Sabbath was to serve as a reminder to the Jews that they had been slaves in Egypt and were delivered from bondage, not by their own efforts, but by the supernatural power of God. The sabbath day was given exclusively to the nation of Israel and never to any gentiles. In the New Testament, there is an even clearer purpose of the Sabbath stated. In Colossians 2:16-17, Paul the Apostle reveals that the Sabbath was only a shadow of things to come and is now fulfilled in Christ. Hebrews 4:1-11, talks about a Sabbath rest that is available to, but not necessarily functional in, all New Testament believers. This New Testament Sabbath rest is simply a relationship with God in which we have ceased from doing things by our own efforts and are letting God work through us (Gal. 2:20; Heb. 4:10). The Sabbath is not a day, but rather a relationship with God through Jesus. Rest in His love and let Him live through you today, because you are more than OK in Him.

This rest or relationship refers to an inner posture of trust and quiet confidence in Jesus' finished work and in His ability to give you increase and good success as you go about doing what you need to do. Rest is not sitting around doing nothing and waiting for His blessings to fall into our laps. Beloved, what God doesn't want you to do is worry and do things out of fear. He wants you to rest at Jesus' feet and listen to His words of love and life. Let Him drive out your fears and lead you to good success!

It is finished! Rest! We are complete in Christ Jesus alone and fully restored in our relationship with "Abba" Father...

God has provided a permanent rest for us through the New Covenant. Our promised land is in our relationship with Jesus Christ. Everything is provided in Him. He offers a life of love, joy and peace to all who would receive it. That even in season of presser we can be at rest in Him.

The only way to enter this rest is by faith. In order to rest, we must stop working. It is impossible to experience the abundant life in Christ while we are still trying to make ourselves acceptable before God by our own works. We must believe and trust in what Christ has done for us at the cross. Just as Robert's father made provisions in his last will for Robert's inheritance, God has made us holy and acceptable in His sight through the New Covenant.

Therefore, brothers, since we have confidence to enter the Most Holy Place by the Blood of Jesus, by a new and living way opened for us through the curtain, that is, his Body, and since we have a great priest over the house of God, let us draw near to God with a sincere heart in full assurance of faith, having our hearts sprinkled to cleanse us from a guilty conscience and having our bodies washed with pure water. Let us hold unswervingly to the hope we profess, for he who promised is faithful.

Hebrews 10:19-23

Are you still trying to live the Christian life in your own strength under law? Write down a few areas where you are performing to get the Fathers approval?

God has provided a new and living way whereby we can enter a permanent Sabbath Rest. Are you willing to enter in by faith today? Write down some steps you think you can take to enter His permanent sabbath rest?

HOW DO WE LABOUR TO enter his rest?

The work we rest from is the dead work of trying to earn God's favour.

There remains, then, a Sabbath-rest for the people of God; for anyone who enters God's rest also rests from his own work, just as God did from his. Let us, therefore, make every effort to enter that rest, so that no one will fall by following their example of disobedience. (Heb 4:9-11)

Read the passage in context of chapter 4 in Hebrews you will see that it is referring to the unbelieving children of Israel. They tried to earn what God wanted to give them freely and consequently they never entered the Lord's rest.

If you don't believe that God wants to bless you and, indeed, that he already has blessed you with every blessing in Christ Jesus, then you will work and never rest. You will exhaust yourself trying to get what he has already given. You may work for salvation, sanctification (holiness), and even a reward, but if you are trying instead of trusting you will be anxious and insecure. Never knowing where you stand with Him. You will always wonder, have I done enough?

Some might say it was because "They didn't keep God's law. You've got to strive and work to keep the commands." Under old law-keeping covenant this was absolutely true, but under the new covenant the only real work is that which flows out of faith in Jesus Christ (see ref. John 6:29).

The issue is not what you do but what you believe, because what you do follows what you believe. Disobedience is a fruit not a root. The Israelites' problem was not that they broke the rules but that they distrusted God:

For we also have had the gospel preached to us, just as they did; but the message they heard was of no value to them, because those who heard did not combine it with faith. (Heb 4:2)

Faith does not compel God to forgive us or sanctify us. Faith doesn't make God do anything. Rather, faith is a positive response to what God has done. Faith is acknowledging every good thing that is already ours in Christ (2 Pet 1:3).

Faith doesn't make things real that weren't real to begin with, but faith makes them real to you. For instance, if you battle with guilt and condemnation, you don't need Jesus to come and take away your sin. You need to believe he already did. Jesus is the cure for guilt, but until you believe it, you won't be cured. Faith is a noun (place, person, or a thing).

Faith is not work, faith is a rest. Faith is a noun, not a verb. Faith is a persuasion that God is who he says he is, has done what he said he's done, and will do what he has promised to do. Consider Abraham, who...

...did not waver through unbelief regarding the promise of God, but was strengthened in his faith and gave glory to God, being fully persuaded that God had power to do what he had promised. (Rom 4:20-21)

Faith is being fully persuaded. When you are fully persuaded, you can rest. The issue is settled. Your mind is made up and your heart is at ease.

If you do not trust God to take care of you and provide for your needs, you will work. Far better to labour towards a place of trust where you cease from your dead works and allow your heart to be established in true righteousness bearing fruit. Do you see? You don't work to earn rest but to enter his rest. Big difference.

Historical evidence regarding the day of Worship.

There is zero historical fact that Christians kept a sabbath day. Rather there is overwhelming evidence of Believers keeping the first day of the week. What we call Sunday. The Apostles in 33 AD were already worshiping on the first day of the week. (Sunday).

Acts 20:7 On the first day of the week, we gathered with the local believers to share in the Lord's Supper. Paul was preaching to them, and since he was leaving the next day, he kept talking until...

1 Cor 16:1-2 Now about the collection for the Lord's people: Do what I told the Galatian churches to do. 2 On the first day of every week, each one of you should set aside a sum of money in keeping with your income, saving it up, so that when I come no collections will have to be made.

150AD JUSTIN: Moreover, all those righteous men already mentioned [after mentioning Adam. Abel, Enoch, Lot, Noah, Melchizedek, and Abraham], though they kept no Sabbaths, were pleasing to God; and after them Abraham with all his descendants until Moses... And you [fleshly Jews] were commanded to keep Sabbaths, that you might retain the memorial of God. For His word makes this announcement, saying, "That you may know that I am God who redeemed you." (Dialogue With Trypho the Jew, 150-165 AD, Ante-Nicene Fathers, vol. 1, page 204)

200AD TERTULLIAN: Let him who contends that the Sabbath is still to be observed a balm of salvation, and circumcision on the eighth day because of threat of death, teach us that in earliest times righteous men kept Sabbath or practiced circumcision, and so were made friends of God...Therefore, since God originated Adam uncircumcised, and inobservant of the Sabbath, consequently his offspring also, Abel, offering Him sacrifices, uncircumcised and inobservant of the Sabbath, was by Him commended... Noah also, uncircumcised - yes, and inobservant of the Sabbath - God freed from the deluge. For Enoch, too, most righteous man, uncircumcised and inobservant of the Sabbath, He translated from this world... Melchizedek also, "the priest of most high God," uncircumcised and inobservant of the Sabbath, was chosen to the priesthood of God. (An Answer to the Jews 2:10; 4:1, Ante-Nicene Fathers Vol. 3, page 153)

220 AD Origen "Hence it is not possible that the [day of] rest after the Sabbath should have come into existence from the seventh [day] of our God. On the contrary, it is our Savior who, after the pattern of his own rest, caused us to be made in the likeness of his death, and hence also of his resurrection" (Commentary on John 2:28).

225 AD The Didascalia "The apostles further appointed: On the first day of the week let there be service, and the reading of the Holy Scriptures, and the oblation, because on the first day of the week our Lord rose from the place of the dead, and on the first day of the week he arose upon the world, and on the first day of the week he ascended up to heaven, and on the first day of the week he will appear at last with the angels of heaven" (Didascalia 2).

250AD CYPRIAN: The eight day, that is, the first day after the Sabbath, and the Lord's Day." (Epistle 58, Sec 4)

The first historical record of methodical Sabbath Keeping by Christians who stopped worshipping on the first day of the week, was two active Anabaptist leaders, Andreas Fisher, and Oswald Glait, became the pioneer and promoters of the Sabbath in 1527 AD.

The reason why believer chose to worship on Sunday (although every day is a good day to) was because Jesus arose on the first day of the week, the Sunday.

<u>Additional reading.</u>

But what about doing the work of God?

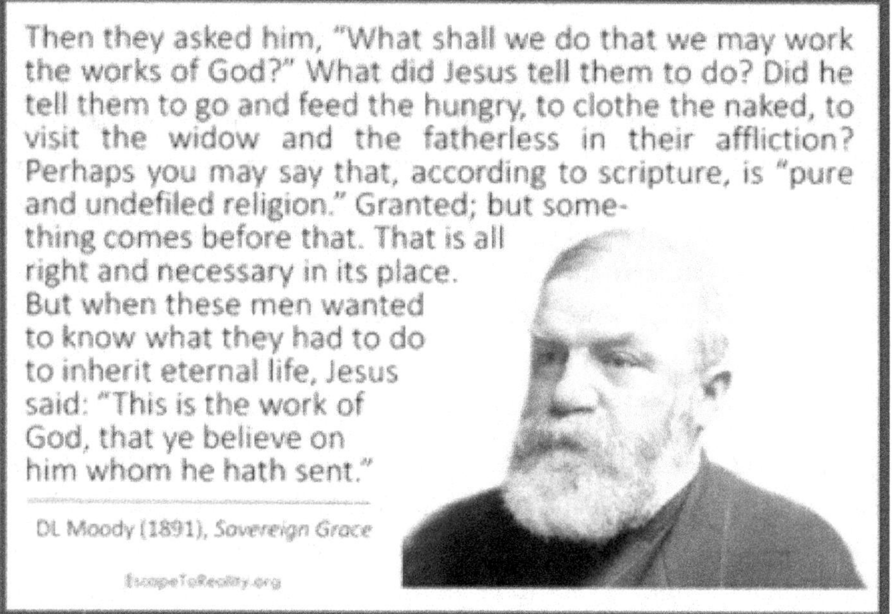

John 6:28 Then they said to Him, "What shall we do, that we may work the works of God?" 29 Jesus answered and said to them, "This is the work of God, that you believe in Him whom He sent."

When you have seen the beauty of Jesus, faith comes easily. Unbelief is the harder choice. To fold your arms and lock your jaw as the goodness of God assails you from every direction requires real commitment.

Unbelief is not passive ignorance. Unbelief is hardening your heart to the manifest goodness of God. Unbelief is cursing that which God has blessed and hating that which he loves. Unbelief is resisting the Holy Spirit and clinging to worthless idols (Acts 7:51, 14:15, 19:9).

I am not talking about people who haven't heard the gospel. I'm talking about those who encountered the love and grace of God and have rejected it. Instead of opening the door to the One who knocks (easy), they've locked it.

Look at how unbelief is described in the New Testament, and you will find plenty of verbs or action words. Unbelief is *rejecting* Jesus (John 3:36) and *denying* the Lord (Jude 1:4). It's *thrusting away* the word of God and *judging* yourself unworthy of life (Acts 13:46). It's *suppressing* the truth (Rom 1:18) and *delighting* in wickedness (2 Th 2:12). It's *turning away* (Heb 12:25), *going astray* (2 Pet 2:15), and *trampling* the Son of God underfoot (Heb 10:29).

And how does Jesus describe unbelievers? As evil*doers* and *workers* of iniquity (Mat 7:23).

Do you see? It takes hard work to succeed as an unbeliever. You need to apply yourself with religious dedication. It's a life-time commitment with no days off. You cannot afford to drop your guard even for a moment or Jesus might sneak up and hug you. If faith is a rest, unbelief is restlessness:

And to whom sware he that they should not enter into his rest, but to them that believed not? So, we see that they could not enter in because of unbelief. (Heb 3:18-19, KJV)

CHAPTER TWELVE

———

G race based Discipleship!

Matthew 28:16-20 "Then the eleven disciples went to Galilee, to the mountain where Jesus had told them to go. When they saw him, they worshiped him; but some doubted. Then Jesus came to them and said, "All authority in heaven and on earth has been given to me. Therefore, go and make disciples of all nations, baptizing them in the name of the Father and of the Son and of the Holy Spirit, and teaching them to obey everything I have commanded you. And surely, I am with you always, to the very end of the age."

John 8:31-32 "To the Jews who had believed him, Jesus said, "If you hold to my teaching, you are really my disciples. Then you will know the truth, and the truth will set you free."

Matthew 4:19-20 "Jesus called out to them, "Come, follow me, and I will show you how to fish for people!" And they left their nets at once and followed him."

2 Timothy 2:2 "You have heard me teach things that have been confirmed by many reliable witnesses. Now teach these truths to other trustworthy people who will be able to pass them on to others."

Definition of disciple: a learner, pupil. Transliteration: mathétés (math-ay-tes') and is a noun. Translated 263 times by Strong's concordance.

If you were to ask the average Christian how disciples are made, the conversation most likely turns to a small group gathering. "We have small connect or cell groups that meet throughout the week or every other week." While disciples are made in community, that's not the extent of disciple making.

A bit of Background. It was customary under the Jewish belief system that the Rabbis would have disciples (learners, pupils) Hence one would say I am a disciple of Joseph or Mark etc. After the book of Acts the word disciple is not found in the original language in the epistles. Rather the emphasis is on being sons (daughters too) of God. Saying that, a disciple is much more than simply a learner and will be sharing a different perspective. Let's look at disciples from a first century Jewish perspective.

First century Jewish education had several levels unlike that of our western education systems. Children begin their study around the age of five or six in Beth Sefer (which means "House of the Book"). At this level teaching focused primarily on Torah (the first five books of the Bible).

For the next four to five years, these young children would memorize large portions of Scripture. In fact, some students memorized the entire Torah by the time Beth Sefer ended at age 10!

After Beth Sefer, most of the students stayed at home to help in the family business. Parents wanted to make sure their kids were well prepared for the future. They felt that two points of education were necessary: <u>understanding of Scripture and training in a vocation</u>. The best students continued their study of Scripture (while learning a trade) in Beth Talmud (House of Learning).

In Beth Talmud, the educational process was much more intense. They studied the Prophets and the Writings in addition to Torah. They learned the interpretations of the Oral Torah (legal and interpretative traditions). They learned how to interpret and apply the Scriptures. They also learned the Jewish art of questions and answers.

———————

THIS SECOND LEVEL OF education focused on understanding deeper truths while **developing critical thinking skills.** And this is one vital difference to Western education which focuses on the exchange of information and the function of memorization. Example, we ask questions like, "What is two plus two?" We want our children to answer "four." Our western educational process is designed around the teacher or facilitator giving information and the student giving it back.

In Jesus' day, the rabbis (priests) taught kids to answer with a question. The focus was not on the exchange of information; <u>the focus was on the understanding of that information</u>. The rabbi might say what is two and two? Instead of answering, "four," the student might say, "What is eight minus four, or what is 25% of 16?" See the difference.

If the student could give the answer in the form of a question, the teacher knew they had processed the information. Jesus was at this stage when His parents lost Him in the temple at the age of 12 (Luke 2:46). It says, "...they found Him in the temple, sitting in the midst of the teachers, both listening to them and asking them questions. And all who heard Him were astonished at His understanding and answers." They were not astonished at his questions. They were astonished at His understanding and answers. **His questions demonstrated His understanding of truth!**

At the end of Beth Talmud, most kids did not continue their education. However, some of the most advanced students would continue to the next level of education called Beth Midrash (House of Study). When students entered Beth Midrash, they were called "talmidim", which is translated "disciples."

At this level, a student would present himself to a Rabbi. The student would say, "Rabbi, I want to become one of your talmidim. Please let me in your House of Study." The Rabbi would ask several questions to evaluate their level of education and understanding. The student had to know if the verse applied to the subject, or was the subject connected to the verse before or after the verse he quoted. Without the Scriptures in front of them, that student had to know the verse, the surrounding verses, the context of those verses, and then tell if the verse was quoted properly for interpretation.

The disciples under the old law-based system goal was simple: He wanted to be like his rabbi. Luke 9:40 says, "Students are not greater than their teacher. But the student who is fully trained will become like the teacher" (NLT). The disciples mimicked everything the rabbi did. This is what the old covenant mindset of a disciple entailed. Under the new covenant we have been made like Jesus spiritually

To be a disciple is more than claiming to be a Christian, attending church, wearing Jesus sandals, and learning Bible stories. It's more than being an admirer of His life or His teachings. It is to be infatuated by His love for you. And not be moved from the truth that "I am the disciple whom Jesus loves."

The wrong ways to approach discipleship. The wrong way to do discipleship is based on fear and pride. Th goal. This kind of behavioural compliance, while seeming good on the surface, is superficial and ultimately does not work to change us at our core. We see Jesus as a pattern to be followed. Seeing Jesus as a mere teacher. It`s about producing fruit in the disciple. Accountability circles which is purely sin focused.

The right way to approach discipleship. The right way to change is to change out of experience of God's grace by knowing Him. To behold Jesus and ourselves in the Word. To understand that we are growing into practical transformational as we keep on beholding Jesus. For as He is, so are we in the world. (see ref. 1 John 4:17). Knowing that this transformation took place in our spirit-man and we need to renew our minds to who`s and who we are. The avenue to lead you into sonship.

The Father is calling us to move from a life based on the law to a life based on grace in every way. Jesus' teaching, life, and death on the cross centred on the movement from living by the law to living by the Spirit of His grace. We see Jesus as the saviour for every day. Only once you know and experience His love can one mimic Jesus correctly. It`s about bearing fruit. Bearing one another burdens, coming along side and encouraging, remind others to be Whom the Father has made them to be.

"A disciple is not one who pursues or follows Jesus in order to become like Him. After the cross, after the resurrection and after the New Covenant began, a disciple is one who believes in Christ and who has been changed by God, is now compatible with God, and who is now led by God from within. The work upon the disciple is done; it is complete. The work within the disciple—where the kingdom is—goes on." Ralph Harris

Following Christ is not complicated. Jesus is God. Jesus fulfilled the Law fully. His yoke is easy and His burden is light (Matthew 11:28–30). We do not obey the Law to be right with God; we have been made right with God by our High priest (rabbi). You abide in Him. As you journey growing into who you are in Him and He in you, you will start to experience what is already a reality inwardly in your born-again spirit man and you will start to experience His life through you outwardly!

<u>The Attributes of a disciple/sons (daughters too)</u>

When people pursue Christ by knowing they are loved they love God, they unite with fellow believers, they impact the world, and they share the good news of the Grace of God.

Love, Unite, Impact, Share.

LOVE

• Enjoying intimate fellowship with God • Getting to know God through His Word • Talking with God • Spending time with God • Worshipping and Praising Him

Unite

• Christian community: In the New Testament, believers enjoyed life together. Jesus and Paul the Apostle travelled with their disciples, had meals together, served together, studied Scripture together, etc. They spent time with each other • They were not just gathering in groups; they were united around common goals and purposes. • Genuine love: Love for other believers and sinners alike defined people as Christ's disciples. They carried each other burdens.

IMPACT

• Showing people love through our actions—not just our words. Faith in action • Following Christ's example of serving others • Investing in people, families, communities, and nations.

Sharing

• Sharing the Gospel of His Grace • Entrusting the teachings of the revelation of the Apostle to Christ finished work to others • Demonstrating the Gospel not only in Word but by Power • Duplication: disciples-making sons and daughters.

<u>Disciples (sons) love, unite, impact, and share the good news of the Gospel by</u> **<u>WORD, POWER, and DEED!</u>**

From the four points mention above there is one common element required; time. Everyone's journey with God is going to look a little different, but we are all on the adventure of a lifetime and that is the same.

The four-point description can serve as a spiritual compass of sorts. If you want to make sure that the course of your life is moving towards growth, place these truths over your life and ask God to reveal the course corrections that need to be made. After all He is the ultimate GPS. Knowing we are Loved by God and loving Him must remain our "spiritual north." Everything else flows out of intimacy with Him.

If you find yourself at a possible spiritual plateau, ask, "What's missing practically?"

Our prayer is that this can provide immediate insights into your journey with God. It can help you see the actionable steps that are needed.

Questions

Question 1. What is the definition of a disciple?

Question 2. Jewish Parents felt that two points of education were necessary. What are they?

Question 3. What is one major difference in education lacking in the western education system?

Question 4. Complete the following statement. The focus was not on the ; the focus was .

Question 5. Complete the following statement. I am the disciple whom Jesus ."

Question 6. Complete the following statement. When people pursue Christ by knowing they are loved they love God, .

Question 7. True or False. The Word disciple is mentioned throughout the New Testament?

Question 8. Duplication is?

Question 9. How do we share the good news of the Gospel?

Question 10. What are the four attributes of the making of a disciple?

No matter where you are Disciples bring the kingdom!

Answers

Answer 1. A pupil or learner.

Answer 2. Understanding of Scripture and training in a vocation.

Answer 3. Critical thinking.

Answer 4. The focus was not on the exchange of information; the focus was on the understanding of that information.

Answer 5. Loves.

Answer 6. When people pursue Christ by knowing they are loved they love God, they unite with fellow believers, they impact the world, and they share the good news of the Grace of God.

Answer 7. False.

Answer 8. Disciples- making sons and daughter.

Answer 9. By Word, Power, and Deed.

Answer 10. Love. Unite. Impact and share.

CONCLUTION

CONGRATULATIONS! YOU have reached the end of this 12-weeks. Now what?

For those interest look out for a ONE-YEAR Foundations course.

Thank you very much for allowing me the honor and privilege to share the beauty of Jesus with you.

Love and rooting for you all.

Paul

ABOUT THE AUTHOR

Paul de Sousa is a Is a son of God. Teacher and A serial entrepreneur. Paul shares his thoughts and insights on several social media platforms reaching tens of thousands weekly.

His Material has reached over 1 million monthly via email. Thanks to the generous donations of believers.

His first and #1 Amazon Best Seller in Four categories The Entrepreneurs Blueprint: Think it, Fund it, Built it, Sell it!

His second and #1 Amazon Best Seller in Four categories: and first in the series in Biblical Foundation an 8- Week Course

Available on amazon and all other good bookstores.

BOOKS by the AUTHOR

Entrepreneurs Blueprint: Think It, Fund It, Build It, Sell It!

Warning: The contents of this book can dramatically help you start your business, grow your sales, create enduring scale, and change your life forever.

If you want serious results and are sick and tired of trying and banging your head on an immovable wall, then this book is a must-listen.

Learn the pro tips, strategies, tactics, and resources of the incredibly successful entrepreneurs, founders, innovators, managers, and businesses on the planet for faster and more reliable revenue to help you realize un- dreamed-of success!

With resources like a 10,000 investors and funders de- tailed database, free accounting software, a list of 90+ free templates, and so much more within the resource took kit.

These pro tips, strategies, tactics, and resources, and a clear blueprint to how to Think It, Built It, Fund It, and Sell It!

Here's a little of what you'll learn:

- Learn the how to and vital importance of canvas model- ling your idea.

- Learn how to sell more and drive more hot traffic through not only normal channels like Facebook but even more effective alternatives.

-Learn how to build a loyal fan base for your brand that can generate epic sales.

-How to build a highly saleable business with access to financial and distribution resources

-Learn the basics of financials and get a list of key financial numbers you got to know if you want to grow, scale, and exit

-Critical sales tools for eCommerce and brick and mortar to a possible eight-figure revenue

-And so much more.

In this book there are summary stories from top entrepreneurs, founders, and start-ups who had major breakouts.

So, if you're a serious entrepreneur who wants the right tools to take it to the next level, then the Entrepreneurs Blueprint is a must-have essential resource tool!

Foundations 8-Week Bible Course

Do you have questions about God, the Bible, and your Christian walk? Have you ever had trouble understanding what the Word says when you read it? If so, internationally recognized Bible teacher Paul de Sousa has developed an amazing and essential tool for you.

In this Foundations 8-week Bible Study Course, you will find answers to questions such as:

-Who You really Are? the answer might change your des- tiny.

-What is Eternal Life? the answer might surprise you. -What is the Goal of it all? the answer most seek.

-How to read my bible correctly and effectively? might surprise in the best of ways.

-What are the baptisms spoken of in the Bible? yes, there are more than one. Surprise.

-What is the New Covenant and why is it vital to know and understand? this is very revelation to deal with... -How do I labor into entering God's Rest? yes, it might sound like a contradiction but it's not.

-Church. Is it for me? Is it needed? With drop in attendances around the world could this be the key.

Even if you have never read the Bible before, you will find this systematic easy to read and practical study guide easy to use and critically beneficial.

If you have been a believer for many years, or just recently you will find a new ease in conversing with God, enjoying fellowship with other Christians, receiving guidance, and witnessing. Through this study, you will experience important changes in your life and discover an intimacy with God that you may never have known before.

To simplify the Word and uncover what it means to you!

Don't miss out!

Visit the website below and you can sign up to receive emails whenever Paul de Sousa publishes a new book. There's no charge and no obligation.

https://books2read.com/r/B-A-XBRV-YKDQC

BOOKS 2 READ

Connecting independent readers to independent writers.